i

On Grölle, (the grey stallion) Whiskers (the baby Grivet Monkey), Coneetcha (the puppy) and Daphne are off to visit a friend who lives down the road. The animals are mentioned in the book.

EXCITEMENTS

IN

ETHIOPIA

CONTENTS

 page

Attempted *Coup d'Etat* (December 1960)........................ 1

Climbing the highest mountain in Ethiopia 51

Small Excitements 137

Mathilda cooks the Curate 176

A fashionable Ethiopian sunshade (in the 1950s and '60s) made of skilfully-woven split cane.

INTRODUCTION

December 1960 was an eventful time in Addis Ababa. First we had an attempted *Coup d'Etat*. For a few bloody and bitter days battles raged through streets and over mountains. The fighting boomed and bashed on for over a week. It ended with public hangings.

Living in the place where the *Coup* broke out, and where subsequently the battles were hottest, I experienced dramatic days, which I describe briefly in the first part of this book.

It's easy to type words such as: Bang! Clash! Explosion! Death, Corpses, Wounds, Blood... and in these days, when wars are everywhere, we have become immune to their significance. The fear, the destruction, the loss of lives, the horror and gory scenes... all these appalling 2018 commonplaces, induced by combat, today leave readers cold. It's different if you're in the thick of it. So, although the *Coup* may have been mercifully short, waves of shock and terror nevertheless shot through those people who lived through it.

Immediately after the *Coup*, the country was still simmering with various outcomes when I set off, with 3 friends, to cross, in an ancient, temperamental vehicle, the vast and magnificent mountainscapes of then-sparsely-populated Ethiopia. At the time, outside Addis, roads were bad, notoriously vicious bandits proliferated and facilities of any kind were poor or non-existent. Sensible people would not have even contemplated this adventure, but we hoped to reach a place from which we intended to try and climb Ras Dashan, the highest mountain in Ethiopia and tenth highest in Africa. For me this badly-equipped expedition was more stirring than the *Coup*; and the report of the trip, taken almost verbatim from my diary, forms the second part of "Excitements in Ethiopia."

In recounting these events I have included details that are not strictly necessary – such as paragraphs about dog and monkey. I feel that expounding upon the 'dramatis personae' makes the stories more readable.

Sadly I had bought a second hand camera which turned out to be faulty. Remember also that the pictures have faded over the 58 years since they were taken – and on poor quality film, which was all we could get in Ethiopia at the time. Digitising them for this book and desaturating them to turn them into B&W didn't exactly enhance them either! I have nevertheless included some shots, substandard though they are, because they do help readers to understand our experiences. Those snaps which were too indistinct to print I have represented by sketches most of which I did when I was a teenager living in Addis. I hope your imagination is up to the task of visualising what the photos and drawings represent!

The names of places mentioned in 'Small Excitements' were spelled variously when we lived in Ethiopia, and some names have since been changed altogether, so if you hunt for villages or the Ethiopian lakes on a map, you may find different spellings, and even different names, from those that I have used.

In the 'Small Excitements' you are let into the secrets of my family anecdotes. They are completely true; but some are groan-worthy. When you've run out of groans skip quickly to the book's last section.

In the final part of *Excitements in Ethiopia* Mathilda was a mule of great character who really lived in Ethiopia. She and her elderly-lady-owner were equally cantankerous, and as intractable as this story describes. The church didn't have a huge porch and there was no art college in Addis when I lived there, but otherwise Mathilda's story recounts events that actually happened one Christmas in the Addis region. I have given the animal and humans in this story false names.

I hope you enjoy reading these very different chronicles.

An ubiquitous, easily- erected Ethiopian gibbet.

ABOUT THE AUTHOR

Daphne was brought up in the Middle East and in Africa. After boarding school and university in Britain, she taught in Ethiopia, was Head of Maths & Science Dept. at Salisbury Polytechnic (Rhodesia), and lectured at the Physics Dept. of University of Rhodesia when it was a college of London University.

She has chosen to put different facts about her life in the 'About the Author' paragraphs in the various books that she has written. Here it seems appropriate to list the times when, *by sheer chance,* she experienced many historical events that could have developed into 'Excitements' of the first water.

In 1952 flying from the UK to Ethiopia entailed a refuelling stop in Rome, where passengers waited in a transit lounge and were offered refreshments. The 20-hour flight paused overnight in Cairo. Passengers, each with only an overnight bag given to them by the airline, were taken to an hotel and returned to the airport the next morning. As a schoolgirl flying home to holidays in Ethiopia, Daphne passed the night in Egyp*t precisely* when King Farouk was deposed. B.O.A.C. passengers knew nothing of these events and were very surprised to be greeted on arrival in Addis Ababa by worried relatives asking how things were in Cairo. Again, Daphne happened to be over-nighting in Cairo when the Suez Crisis erupted. (1956).

In January 1954 she flew via Rome on a Comet. The *very next* Comet flight through Rome exploded in mid air. After piston planes the Comet was superbly smooth, silent and rapid. WONDERFUL! Imagine - There were only 36 passengers *in all*: and everything was very luxurious: meals, seats, rest rooms (hand-creams etc. supplied)...

The family escaped being the first Mau Mau victims thanks to her father's driving skills when, in the Kenyan Highlands in 1952, they met a crowd of screeching, befeathered, spear-waving warriors.

As this book describes she had a breathless few days in Addis during the 1960 attempted *Coup d'état*; and she left Ethiopia at the end of her teaching contract before serious troubles started.

She survived through the start of UDI in Rhodesia and was luckily transferred to Malawi just before the bloody Rhodesian Civil War started.

Again by chance she left Malawi just before things there began to be 'difficult'.

Daphne introduces SOME OTHER DRAMATIS PERSONAE

I acquired Coneetcha – the dog – when I was riding to a rehearsal of 'Charley's Aunt'. A muddy bundle lay on the road. It moved. It was a puppy! So I called to the man standing by the nearest mud-and-thatch hut to tell him that one of his pups had strayed.
"Oh, no," he replied. "We put it on the road because it's a bitch. She'll be run over, or the hyenas will get her tonight."
For obvious reasons I called her 'Coneetcha Shunta' ('Flea Bag' in Amharic). She probably stocked the hall with 'bighties' while spending the rehearsal in a cardboard box.

The ex-Flea-Bag became a great companion who, during a long lifetime, travelled with me in a VW Beetle round much of Africa. She was unfazed driving from Ethiopia down to Rhodesia – which needed a compass on some stretches. Crossing Kenya, she wore a big sombrero through Game Parks where only elephants rumbled her disguise. Growling threateningly they moved en masse towards us. Coneetcha and I camped just about everywhere in Rhodesia and South Africa. Finally, together we drove up to Malawi and got to know most of the Malawian roads and mountains.

There are details about Grölle and Whiskers in the following stories.

- - - - - - - - - - -

Unless stated otherwise photos in this book were taken by me or by members of my family. Sketches are my teenage, and later, attempts at recording life in Addis Ababa.

The cover has a picture of the Lion of Judah statue in Addis Ababa.

THE 1960 ATTEMPTED ETHIOPIAN *COUP D'ETAT*

MY OWN EXPERIENCES – NOT A HISTORICAL REPORT.

1

H.I.M. Haile Selassie at a ceremony in the Jubilee Palace before the terrible *Coup*.

The Emperor couldn't live in the Jubilee Palace after the atrocities that were enacted there at the start of the *Coup*. He gave it to the University.

The 'Lion of Judah,' (Haile Selassie) had lions 'everywhere'. Presumably the carved example at the top of the steps didn't object to the soldier who stood beside him at sunrise and sunset to raise and lower the flag; but the Emperor's two young, pet lions, that used to roam freely in the Palace gardens, weren't so tolerant. The creatures didn't like white faces.

Before the gory events Mr and Mrs Jary, who looked after the youngest members of the Imperial family and tutored them, lived in the Palace grounds. After a few frightening encounters with the young lions, Mrs Jary plucked up courage to inform the Emperor of the situation. This was a delicate matter for the Ethiopians spoke of *themselves* as 'white' and she nearly 'put her foot in it' by saying:

"Your Majesty, your lions don't like – er - whi – er –foreigners."

A compromise was reached whereby Jarys and lions didn't have to come face to face.

3

SETTING THE SCENE:

I was 23 years old and teaching at The Empress Menen Secondary School for girls in Addis Ababa. From an Ethiopian gentleman I rented an ancient but convenient bungalow with a paddock where my horses and dog could gambol. My lodger, Karen, a year or two older than me, worked at the University College – also not far away; but she and I headed off in different directions to get to work.

Our cottage was in a wooded dell, lower than the lane which separated it from the imposing walls of the Crown Prince's palace. My Grivet monkey (Whiskers) used to make short work of those august and forbidding ramparts. If he could get loose he rushed straight for His Imperial Highness's forest of tall, lush trees. Then, clutching a tempting banana, I had to walk round and beg the guards to let me in so that I could catch Whiskers before he got into mischief inside the palace *buildings*!

To left and right of our humble house extended a long muddle of circular, thatched, Ethiopian huts called called *toukuls*. Our bungalow *wasn't* round. Neither was it thatched. Its corrugated iron

roof was an excellent thermometer as it CLANGED loudly every time the temperature rose or fell, making the sheets of iron change size and buckle or unbuckle. However, like the *toukuls*, our home *did* have mud walls, which made it super-easy to position nails as picture hooks! During the attempted revolution the walls also absorbed bullets very efficiently.

Whiskers, one of Coneetcha's pups and I go for a ride.

In the garden, close behind the house, were two mud-and-wattle quarters in which my servants and their families survived.

Facing our bungalow lived the Emperor's caged lions beside a triangular patch of short coarse grass. That patch extended into just vacant meadowland where alone, and virtually unused, a roundabout rotated apparently in the middle of nothingness. I drove across that arid area on my way to and from work every day.

A shamma = a universally worn, toga-like shawl made of white, gauzy material. Some *shammas* had splendid, colourful borders.

Above: Our milk arrived in tins that had originally held motor oil. Pasteurisation?... What was that? Cattle TB? ... Never heard of it! Hygiene?... We had to be tough in Addis.
Note the milkman's modest *shamma*. From time to time I dipped a thermometer into the milk and sternly ordered the man to stop watering it. Then, for a while, the milk was rich again.
Left: A fine guy wearing a very smart *shamma*. with a colourful, shiny border.

Beyond the rough ground stood the Imperial Guards' Barracks, the Ministry of Finance and, a little further on, the Jubilee Palace: – all strategic places during the *Coup*.

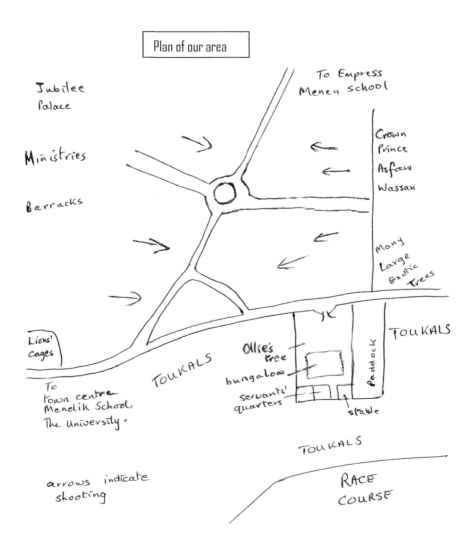

Plan of our area

Dotted everywhere round Addis tall clumps of gum trees wrapped the definitive Eucalyptus perfume of the city round palaces, hovels, ordinary homes, lions' cages and government buildings.

A man wearing a *shamma* passes in front of the Commercial Bank. The lion statue, which is sporting an Ethiopian crown, has been outlined to emphasise it. I was told that before wisdom prevailed the tail had a light bulb at its tip ! The car on the ramp was being raffled.

Three women wearing *shammas* and gauzy head-scarves. From left to right the dress/ *shammas'* borders are: a very broad deep green; no edging; and a turquoise design. The head coverings are black, kingfisher-blue, and ruby. (Only prostitutes wore red scarves. Brothels were legal, accepted, and often run by respected, high-class ladies)

7

THE FIRST SOFT RUMBLES

"Addis Ababa
20th December 1960

Dear Mother and Dad,

You will have heard on the BBC about the attempted Coup d'Etat that has just taken place in Addis. Terrible things happened: innocent people died; homes were destroyed; buildings burnt. The troubles climaxed with public hangings.

I am extremely sad to tell you that Lij Makonnen Hapte Mariam, that fine, cultured diplomat, who was so huge and handsome, is dead. With other noblemen he was tricked into the Jubilee Palace on the evening of Tuesday, December 13th and, a short time later, mown down in cold blood by machine guns. It doesn't bear thinking about. All of them – so many our friends – just massacred! Lij Makonnen was such a splendid person, so magnificent in his Ethiopian dress of white shamma and jodhpurs, and – apart from the superb aspects of his character – such an expert on the dance floor that it was not only an honour but also sheer pleasure to dance with him at the Palace Balls.

As far as we expatriates were concerned the Coup began almost inconspicuously. It (whatever that was) started the day after the massacre, which was, as yet, not known to the public. I noticed that the Palace Guards didn't afflict our eardrums by their daily custom of getting the most from their trumpets and drums as they marched along our lane. En route to duty at the Emperor's palace, they usually stomped past our cottage at breakfast time, more or less in step, puttees dazzling white, instruments gleaming and drummers decorated with leopard skins... Why did they go to all that trouble? Only sleepy

Louries

mongrels and frightened chickens noticed the daily strident passage. Maybe colourful Louries in the luscious tops of those exotic trees within the Crown Prince's grounds flapped gorgeous crimson wings, peered down over the very high never-ending walls, and cackled harshly and crossly at the disturbance.

Since the Guardsmen were frequently very late I thought nothing of the musicians' absence and was merely glad that they hadn't impeded my daily 08.10 uphill exit from the garden. That morning, on my 4-minute dash to school, I noticed a couple of armoured cars squatting in the waste land. For some months miscellaneous warlike vehicles had appeared with increasing frequency outside the Emperor's palace and that of his son, the Crown Prince Asfaw Wassan, so I assumed that today these were simply, 'practising tactics, pretending to defend important buildings.' How revolting they looked, with their vicious guns obscenely threatening the world. They crouched evilly, partially hidden in the long grass, as lethal as African ticks in a dog's hair. I had no premonition that the next day (Thursday 15th December) I would be dodging bullets as I crossed this empty expanse.

During morning break on Wednesday, my pupils jostled fiercely to claim places from which they could look over the school walls but, to preserve my dignity, I didn't reveal my curiosity by joining them. Their excitement soon fizzed over:
"Oh, Miss! Soldiers!"
"They're right round the Emperor's palace, Miss; and they've blocked off all roads on that side of the school."
"Oh, Miss!"
In the staffroom we found these strange antics puzzling but who were we to quibble if "Military Manoeuvres" were in progress?

At noon, Michel Houdrey arrived from the University College with shocking news. There had been a Coup d'État. The head of the College had sent his staff to collect their wives and children from where ever they might be.
Michel removed his wife, and as soon as I could leave school, I drove into town. Luckily I had been paid on Monday so I filled my car and a spare jerry can with petrol and spent Eth$32 (then about GB£7.5) on

tinned food, rice, flour, lentils etc, just in case they might be needed. There wasn't a crumb of bread to be had anywhere. Abata and I exchanged news through our cars' open windows as we drove twice round the Piazza. It was squirming with pedestrians and vehicles that seemed to have gone berserk. Seicientos (small communal taxis) dodged, zig-zagging, through a mêlée of frantic vehicles like demented water beetles on a dark, turbulent pond. Over-excited gharry horses, sensing something in the air, were difficult to manage and got in everyone's way. But despite the movement all seemed strangely subdued – perhaps ominously so.

After lunch many pupils were missing. The others couldn't settle so Princess Ruth (The Emperor's granddaughter and our headmistress) allowed them to dismiss. She was (or rather, I trust – still is) such a nice person, and great fun on informal occasions such as riding picnics and gymkhanas. That Wednesday she was unapproachable, brusque and worried. Subsequently she was not seen, and later, having heard of the grisly events in the palace, we became very concerned about what might have happened to her."

Although Princess Ruth was probably preoccupied by information that was not yet common knowledge, ordinary folk still had no idea of the horrific massacre, or of dangers which lay in store; so that evening a cosmopolitan bunch enjoyed the usual exhilarating Wednesday tennis at the British Embassy. Charles failed to materialise. He had turned home after meeting a posse of threatening-looking rebels down by the airport.

However, along *my* way as I tootled up to participate, all was tranquil. Addis was, in those days, a vast sprawling city where a few modern buildings, and some old imposing churches, rose here and there between thousands of *toukuls*. There was plenty of space and lots of 'waste' land where donkeys and cows grazed. Everywhere the ubiquitous gum trees spread a fragrant bluish-green canopy. My route to the Embassy was therefore mainly between *toukuls* where half-naked infants toddled about as their mothers thudded heavy poles to pulverise grain in big wooden mortars. Scratching dogs lay in the dirt. Goats and chickens foraged for whatever they could find, the former often stood (wagging beards disdainfully) on thatched roofs from which Eucalyptus smoke seeped as evening meals were cooked.

Two ladies pounding maize. They take it in turn to thud down into the mortar.

11

Presumably news of the Addis unease hadn't filtered out into the villages because there were still hordes of little donkeys clip-clopping home along the roadsides. Earlier, looking like small, bobbing haystacks, they must have carried enormous loads of hay to the Big Market while, with the bouncing walk of mountain folk, their drovers loped beside them waving sticks and shouting piercingly: "*Go-deen! Go-deen! Go-deen!*" (Keep in! Keep in! Keep off the road!")

Girl on her way to sell Eucalyptus branches as fuel, and milk (in an old oil can).

Women, laden with huge bundles, wobbled from side to side as they plodded stoically, bent almost double, with eyes unavoidably fixed upon their feet. Men, carrying bundles of tremendously long poles on their heads, made a familiar frieze against mountains and mud huts. As their bodies bobbed they generated sine waves along the length of the supple poles and the ends sprang up and down.

This man is taking firewood and empty oil cans to sell in the Addis Big Market.
Note his 'raincoat' hanging over his shoulder. Made of reeds, it can stand up like a small tent.

On the next page are more shots of human beasts of burden.
      1   A woman hurries to the Big Market to sell dung as fuel.
      2   Wearing traditional jodhpurs and tunic a man carries a load of hay.
      3   This chap is hoping to sell some large pots made by his wife.

Roads were always very full – not so much with vehicles as with people, horses, mules and donkeys, all carrying large loads to or from market. Thank goodness a recent edict forced vendors to use cages instead of suspending chickens upside down, strung from poles by their legs, as used to be the custom.

14

At the Embassy, during a pause in the tennis, there was some casual mention of possible 'troubles'. Whatever 'they' meant by 'troubles' that idea seemed completely nebulous. Sipping our freshly-made lemon squash we smiled when Mr Joy, the First Secretary, told us to seek safety in the diplomatic compound if anything blew up. No-one visualised such extreme eventualities. The next selection of tennis partners seemed much more important, and I was preoccupied with wondering what to give visitors for supper.

Karen and I had invited the Hudsons and Ruanpagers to a meal and a game of Buccaneer; but, with troops hanging about, it turned out that our guests were unwilling to venture so close to the Palaces and Ministry of War. Over the phone Mrs Hudson suggested: "Why don't you bring the food that you've prepared round to our place? Don't forget your sleeping bags as well," she added "If trouble breaks out you can stay overnight – away from your hot spot."
There was that word again! 'Trouble' ??? I couldn't believe what was happening. Actually none of us went anywhere because a 7pm-to-6am curfew was imposed.

As usual the BBC didn't come through clearly, but we managed to grasp, at 7pm, a mere mention of Ethiopia. The 9 o'clock news headlined vaguely that something had transpired in Addis. My great concern was for my parents in Cyprus. The unspecific BBC reports would make them worry and, at the moment, no one, not even embassies, appeared to have information which could be relayed to let the outside world know what was happening.

I heard a shot as I was putting the animals to bed. This was disquieting but nothing more happened, though the dark hours were loud with the rumblings of armoured cars and lorries. These gave Karen a horribly anxious night; but there were no other disturbances so I made a stout effort to blot their thunder out of my mind and slept more or less soundly. Our opposite neighbours – the Emperor's caged lions – implied that all was well by, as usual, roaring viciously and frequently during the early hours. As all King of Beasts do, these representatives of H.I.M. Haile Selassie, the Lion of Judah, bellowed tremendously and then chuffed away decrescendo, with echoes rebounding off the walls of the Crown Prince's palace. Karen and I were accustomed to their chants but any visitors used to find their racket frightening and hard to accept.

That – as I said – was Wednesday 14th. The following 15th to 20th were action-packed. For a start here is a bit from my diary.

"Today, 11.30 on Thursday 15th, I am in my lab with the girls doing Physics revision questions. Nothing could appear calmer! But I doubt that the pupils have learnt a thing. Our thoughts are supposedly upon the exams, scheduled to start on December 23rd, and on the end of term – January 6th. We are looking forward to 2 weeks' Christmas holiday which will follow. (You will remember that Ethiopians follow the Coptic calendar so their Christmas falls later than ours.)

However, just outside the school, armoured cars were circling round the Emperor's Palace and others were stationed at tactical points on various roads all about us, each squatting like a tarantula who is contemplating a vast leap. (Do tarantulas leap?) Troops were also hovering further away – all round town.

Beyond the lions' cages, The Ministry of Finance was swarming with soldiers scurrying hither and yon. At the Emperor's Palace, instead of just the customary relaxed couple of men beside the gates, now guns bristled outwards from all sides. – Whatever could that mean? Exactly who the reinforced vehicles and militia were supporting was an open question. Nobody – not even Embassies – could tell us what had happened or what was going on."

There were two current rumours:

1   The Crown Prince had seized power.
2   There had been a *Coup d'etat* organised by Brigadier General Mengistu, head of the Imperial Bodyguard. All the guns were pointing out from the Jubilee Palace because Mengistu had captured two palaces, was holding the Crown Prince prisoner and had forced him, at gunpoint, to broadcast a prepared statement to the effect that he (Asfaw Wassan) had taken over the country. It was said that some of the Imperial Bodyguard and a section of the Police were supporting Mengistu.

The flower of the army was on United Nations duties in the Congo, and the rest of the militia was apparently sitting on the fence.

The local wireless station broadcast that foreigners had nothing to fear. How reliable was that? Who now controlled that

16

radio station? Telephones were dead. Post Office and Bank intermittently operated and closed. Loud speakers that normally broadcast deafening Ethiopian music to the town's main squares fell silent.

We worried about Mr and Mrs Jary inside the Jubilee Palace with the youngest members of the Emperor's family. They were now presumably in Mengistu's power, behind those menacing weapons. We couldn't make contact and had heard nothing of them or of the Imperial children. Prince Paul was a friend of my brother, Christopher. As very little boys they had held hands for security at frightening birthday parties. Paul was many years beyond that stage now; but where was he and what was happening to him?

The Emperor, who had been in Brazil, cut short his State Visit to several South American and African countries, and was expected back at any moment. Would this provoke civil war? Some people, panicking, were buying selfishly large stocks of food from Polyterides', the only grocer in town. Others were camping at the airport hoping to catch the first plane out: a futile hope since there *was* no air traffic of any sort at the moment.

Everywhere a fog of anxiety and uncertainty prevailed. I felt helpless, frozen, worried, and yet I found it difficult to be physically afraid. It was as though I was stuck immobile in a Pending Tray with no control as to whether I escaped or was relegated to OUT or to Dustbin.

The British Embassy was organising with Aden and Nairobi to evacuate us if necessary. I sincerely prayed that it wouldn't happen. Nothing could be worse. For one thing it would mean that there had been dangerous developments and that blood had been shed: a terrifying thought. For another I did *not* want to leave my animals and all my belongings. Of course my meagre possessions were only a millionth, millionth of what some people had to lose…and they were merely *things*. Would *lives* be in danger?

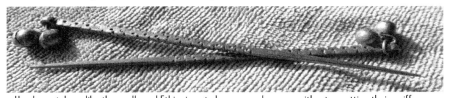

Head scratchers like these allowed Ethiopians to have a good scrape without upsetting their coiffures.

THINGS START TO HAPPEN.
RETREAT TO THE BRITISH EMBASSY

After lunch that Thursday the armoured cars had gone. I rejoiced, thinking that, one way or another, matters had come to a bloodless end; but it was merely a pause while talks were being held. I called my register and then, having no afternoon lessons, and affected by the unquiet atmosphere, I decided to do my marking at home. However, unbeknownst to me, some sort of truce had just ended.

Sure, the armoured cars had gone – but – Bless me!!!! I had reached the 'roundabout-to-nowhere' in the middle of the empty, rough terrain when "BANG!" I thought someone had suffered an extremely loud burst tyre. But my little royal-blue-and-black Austin was the only car in sight... Then I realised:
'Help! That was a rifle shot!'
So I stamped on the gas and circled that *rond point* not only like a rally driver, but also in the wrong direction – to be as far as possible from the Crown Prince's Palace, for it was from out of his gardens that shots were now exploding in rapid succession.

By the time I had reached the bare triangular patch in front of our house the shooting was thick and fast. Ethiopians were cowering all round, hiding in roadside ditches, behind odd rocks, bushes, and in clumps of grass... I looked at them in amazement. Normally this piece of land lay as bare of humans as Macbeth's blasted heath. Then I realised that they were wearing camouflage. They were troops! – carrying weapons! – heading away from the palace and facing others who were even now creeping towards the palace. I nearly expired with fright when I noticed two long rows of armed men all pointing guns, big and small, straight at my car! In fact they must have been aiming at each other *past* my A40 but I was right in the centre of their formations and in their direct lines of fire!

I stopped and crouched below the steering wheel; but after a few moments, which seemed like hours, I couldn't bear the tension. I peered out to see if it would be possible to get home. One of the soldiers saw me peeping and impatiently waved me to:
"Get the Hell out of the way!"
I wasn't calm enough to think coherently but rather, I 'felt':

'Either I proceed slowly, showing them that I am a foreigner, and hoping that their aim is good enough for them to miss me. Or else, for goodness knows how long, I stay bent double in their direct line of fire within the utterly negligible protection of the car.'

Later I heard that an acquaintance, Mon. Leblanc, caught in a similar position, had chosen to stay squatting low in his car. He was killed in the crossfire. His son was wounded in the thigh, and another Frenchman with them, was shot through the stomach. The latter two recovered gradually in hospital.

Moving off seemed the lesser of two evils. I popped up, and drove on. There were bodies on the dirt road and one stretched, but still moving, in the long grass. I barely had the courage to look at them. It flashed upon me: 'the grotesque postures indicate that some, at least, among them are dead.'

It took enormous will power to drive slowly, but the most frightful part came next – when I approached the large, bare, triangular patch in front of our bungalow. I drove at tortoise pace. As it bent, the track then forced me to double back. And, while negotiating *each* section of the 'elbow', I was passing straight across the line of fire. Perhaps I should have reversed rapidly back to school but that option never entered my head. I had just one thought: 'Get home if you can survive that long!'

After the trauma of twice passing directly across the firing line I had to get out of the car to open the garden gate, which was made of 2m-high slats of wood. One wretched, terrified soldier, clasping a machine gun, was concealed in a tree by our entrance. He took the opportunity to rush, between the shots, into the garden. At this juncture Waldi, my outside servant, appeared from behind the house where he had been taking shelter in his quarters. Having heard the approach of my car, he had come to let me in. With astonishing bravery, he grasped the petrified soldier by the shoulders, turned him round, and propelled him out of the gates, which he then very calmly proceeded to close and lock, while I parked the car in the usual place beside the house. I was *most* impressed by Waldi's *sang froid*!

Zeleka, my cook-houseboy, off duty at this hour, was visiting the *toukul* next door but hearing my car, dodging the bullets, and naively holding up a torn piece of old newspaper as protection, he dashed home. Either Waldi and Zeleka were simply unaware of what

19

missiles could do or they were extraordinary conscientious and courageous. Circumstances quickly made them grow up and lose their naiveté.

Waldi and the bigger creatures of my 'menagerie.' Skal, the brown horse, is hiding.

It now penetrated my numbskull that our cottage, though a very humble, uninteresting dwelling, was in a desperately dangerous spot, completely surrounded by palaces, ministries and barracks. A few days ago Yeshi, Waldi's wife, had by chance, gone with her infant daughter and baby son to visit relatives in Gulele, a district on the far western outskirts of Addis. One of the teachers where I worked drove from, and back to, Gulele each day. That morning she had mentioned that everything was completely normal and quiet out there so I decided it would be a Good Idea to make sure that Mrs Waldi didn't return, and to evacuate Mrs Zeleka as well. She wailed and howled saying that she didn't want to leave her home and husband. But Zeleka understood my point and spoke to his wife – Nigatua – kindly and firmly. A biddable girl, still in her teens, she allowed herself to be persuaded, so I hustled them to prepare her bundle of necessities.

We waited till the shooting had lessened and then, giving Mrs Zeleka a few dollars to help her and Yeshi survive at Gulele, I shoved

Nigatua and her baby, Shoala – who bore a lamentable likeness to her father, Zeleka!
Nigatua wears a *shamma* with a splendid broad band, but she couldn't afford a *silky* border.

Nigatua and her baby out of sight on the floor of the car, and perspiring with concentration, drove exceptionally slowly (to show that I was white). That was the first time I ever ground my teeth but the habit of clamping my jaws when stressed has remained with me ever since.

Beyond our neighbourhood far fewer bullets were speeding around. They missed us – whether by luck or by the skill of the army we'll never know. I was terrified: too scared to do more than *glance* at the militia who almost brushed the car as they trudged along the edges of the narrow road using shrubs and trees as cover. They looked so murderous! I became even more frightened when, panic-stricken, Nigatua started wailing again. If she bawled the baby would yell as well, and if her howls came to the soldiers' ears it was ten to one that they'd take a pot shot at the source. I had to be rude and pressurise the girl. But it did the trick. She pulled herself together and, once we had escaped from the region of barracks and palaces, we were out of the shooting.

The crowded, but (mercifully) peaceful, bus stop in town was functioning so I was able to put Nigatua into a queue, hoping that public transport would get her through to Gulele. There she could join Mrs Waldi and tell her that they, and their children, were to remain with Yeshi's relations till sent for – i.e. after the bloody events in our region had subsided back to normal.

There were even fewer guns banging about by the time I returned to the bungalow where I found Karen, jittery, and dithering about what to do. As we had already prepared a few items, and remembering advice from Mr Joy at the Embassy after the tennis session yesterday – Wednesday, I had no hesitation at all about our plan of action. I told her to pack her car and, while she did that, I put my clothes, bedding, camping stuff, and all the food I could possibly find, into my Austin, plus the jerry can of petrol, First Aid kit, etc. Karen was always mocking me for being too tidy and precise, but now it stood me in very good stead. In 10 minutes I was ready – partly because I had had it all planned since last July – 'Just in case'! I have to admit, though, that later I discovered that in the rush I had shoved in some totally useless junk! I also took all my dresses but not a single belt! Loose, beltless clothes were not yet in vogue.

Zeleka grinds coffee beans for me. To show that he, a man, is doing woman's work, he uses only one hand. Maybe making a male mistake, he's got the *up*-end of the pestle *down* in the mortar.

While shots were zinging away not more than ten yards from us Waldi and Zeleka behaved exceptionally, helping us to carry our gear out of the house and then to pack it into the cars. When we had loaded up I gave the servants 23Eth$, which was all that remained in my purse. I asked them to keep alive, if possible, my horses, rabbits, chickens, owl and tortoises that I was not taking with me but to clear out if things became too hot. Easily said, of course; but *how* would they be able to escape? – and where *to*? Gulele was a long way off if war intervened.

There was much coming and going round the Imperial Bodyguard Headquarters, nearly opposite our little bungalow, so we thought things could only go from bad to worse and didn't wait for any definite lulls in the barrage. With Coneetcha, my bitch, balanced quite unperturbed on top of my heap of 'jumble', and Whiskers, the Grivet monkey, cheetering with frenzy, petrified even beyond the stage of wetting, and clinging to me with his ears sticking out, and his eyes as if on stalks, we drove out of the gate, uphill on our tiny drive, and into what we hoped would be a respite in the firing.

As well as *round* our house the shooting seemed to be *behind* it, where the race-course stretched for miles, so I avoided the shorter route which would have gone that way and took the big avenue down past the Menelik School. In fact fighting had started simultaneously in at least six places: The Piazza, The Ministry of War, The Bishoftu Armoury, The Technical College, The University and The Jubilee Palace – our area.

As we passed the University we ran through more firing but it was negligible compared with that round the Palace region. Forcing ourselves to drive slowly, we pressed on towards the very beautiful grounds of the British Embassy on the extreme eastern edge of Addis. It was a long way to the isolated compound, where houses of diplomats and other staff, as well as offices and stables, spread up the slope of the mountain range that borders the north of the city. On the way poor Karen got a shimmy on her steering but she managed to keep driving.

It struck me that our proposed refuge might be rather full, and Mrs Khalil had offered me a room if things became dangerous at our place. She and her family lived just a couple of hundred yards from the theoretically 'British' land, in one of the very few houses along

24

the road to the Embassy, so I thought that the Ambassador's staff might like Karen and me to accept my friend's offer in order to leave more space for other refugees. Having located Mr Joy, who approved of our plan, we installed ourselves in the Khalils' house. All this was over by 4pm but, – by Jove! It seemed as if we'd been on the hop for decades! We settled down to a cup of tea with our hosts and the Dimitris, who were also availing themselves of the Khalils' hospitality. Mrs Khalil and Mrs Dimitri were Domestic Science teachers at the Empress Menen School where I was in charge of Physics. Having been born in Egypt and brought up in the Middle East, I had become very friendly with them and to this day I use their Arab and Greek recipes. {Thank you, ladies!}

Soon we could hear shots even in that area so far out of town. Our hosts panicked. Karen and I felt we had better report once more to the Embassy, where we met a bunch of evacuees like ourselves. Some of them had endured spine-chilling experiences. Ken, an F.A.O. official, was driving through town when he was suddenly surrounded by fast shooting. Coming towards him the driver and passengers in a *seiciento* leapt out of the taxi and disappeared, but left the engine of their vehicle running. The car went smack into Ken's VW. Luckily no one was hurt but, under heavy fire, Ken had to jump out of his car and struggle to dislodge the taxi from his very bent front bumper. With difficulty he then managed to drive out of danger.

Two missionaries despaired when confronted by a huge armoured tank rushing down upon them on the wrong side of a roundabout. The colossus came roaring at their tiny, low-powered 2CV Citroën. Desperate attempts to avoid the thundering monster were useless. The driver's side of their flimsy vehicle was flattened against the solid stone wall that surrounded the central monument. The passenger side was completely ripped away by the passing tank. They were left in a twisted 'cage'. Luckily it was still mobile – just.

Stories such as these shook us. On second thoughts, it seemed better to be actually on official land; and it also appeared as if life among the refugees might be rather fun; so Karen and I decided to transfer to the Embassy. I had expected that we'd be squeezed into Embassy buildings but ample accommodation, in the form of a row of tents, had been set up in the paddock, where we usually enjoyed gymkhanas, fêtes, and similar events.

{The tents were in a line along the course where once, riding side by side, Gebre Selassie, a dark Ethiopian lad, and I, had won a synchronised jumping event in the face of much older and more experienced riders. Gebre Selassie, whose father was one of the Imperial Guards, had been mounted on a huge grey (a milky white Imperial Guards' steed); and I was riding a dainty, but very spirited and pitchy-black, Arab stallion whose nostrils flared crimson. It had been tricky to get our differently-sized mounts to reach the obstacles together and to soar over them simultaneously.}

As we drove back to the Khalils small bombs started plopping down and the main road was now full of troops, straggling along to heaven-knew-where. With the dirt lane up to the Khalils' seething with uniformed fellows, all carrying guns of various sorts, the situation looked horribly threatening. We heard the rumble of approaching tanks. Terrifying! The now-very-scared Khalils were relieved to learn that the British officials wanted us within their grounds – which was 99.9% true – and thought of joining us.

In the *toukuls* behind the Khalils' house a woman was shrieking. The screams were soul-shredding and horrifying: dreadful, penetrating, loudspeaker-sort-of yells, that echoed and re-echoed round the mountainside. I guess she was either undergoing a protracted, difficult childbirth or was being gang raped; but even if they knew what was going on the Khalils would never have spoken of such events; so we didn't find out what was causing the woman's agony, and even had we been able to reach her, there was nothing we could have done to stop her anguish. It was nightmarish to drive away with those screeches filling the valley.

In twelve horror-stricken minutes we had again loaded pets and baggage into cars and driven like fiends back to the British Embassy, weaving our shuddering vehicles through dozens of armed desperados who reluctantly moved sluggishly out of our way. The impressively-turbaned Sudanese guards at the Embassy entrance, much bigger than Ethiopians, were presumably chosen for their size and courage, and usually they conveyed a powerful sense of security. But today we viewed them dubiously and sympathetically. What would those stalwarts be able to do if the Ethiopian soldiers, who, like columns of warrior ants, were spilling along the road, decided to turn in through the Embassy gates? No matter how valiantly the defenders fought they'd quickly be reduced to minced meat.

Karen and I were thankful to arrive unharmed and were allocated one of the tents. Sharing our canvas home were two nursing sisters who had been in town. Unable to make their way back to the Tsehai Hospital, they had been forced, by advancing troops, to retreat to the Embassy. As I pumped up the air mattress that I had brought with me I wondered how safe we would be under such flimsy 'protection'. It had never occurred to anyone that safety seekers would be lodged in *tents*!

That night we numbered about twenty refugees. We ate gratefully in various houses on the Embassy compound. Three lecturers from the College were installed under canvas next to us. They had been in the University when noisy firing made them seek protection in the cellar. From there they had watched a bomb land on a house which thereupon disintegrated. A tank bullet entered through the back windscreen of Roy's car and emerged via the radiator but the engine still worked so, at the first lull, these three lecturers made a dash for the British Embassy. Of course neither the hospital sisters nor the lecturers had been able to bring blankets or food so Karen and I lent them both for we had plenty.

MORTARS ABOVE AND BELOW

Except for random intermittent shots the refugees' first **night (of Thursday 15th)** was calm – until about 5.15 am. Then 'They' started using mortars. *We* didn't know who 'They' were and 'They' didn't know how to aim – or perhaps they simply didn't know *who* they were supposed to be aiming *at*! The mortar shells seemed to be directed at the hill immediately behind us. Some landed, with nasty !*!CRUMPS!*!, unpleasantly close to our tents. A number of rifle bullets came cracking into the trees of a small wood just above us. Have you had experience of little bombs being thrown at you at random like hundreds and thousands being scattered over a cake? It's not at all amusing!

After half an hour of this we had had enough. Karen and I, plus the nurses, decamped, with our bedding, into the Residency where we lay on the hall floor. Other people went into the Joys' house. Now I knew why the Residency (the Consul's office and house) was built so stoutly. I had always wondered why its walls were made of such strong stonework and why one had to climb steep stairs to reach its defendably-high front door. In chilly pre-dawn it was extremely comforting to climb those robust steps and disappear out of the rain of shells behind a thickly reinforced wooden door.

At breakfast time, being served coffee and toast by uniformed Residency servants at a table spread with a linen cloth we made diplomatic, polite conversation with Mr Peel, the Consul.

A stray reporter who was in Addis when the balloon went up had appeared to take refuge at the Embassy. He wasn't a bit excited about sharing breakfast with diplomats or by the scoop that being on the spot at this historic moment should have given him. He was, however, very interested in my pets, Whiskers and Coneetcha. He took several photos of them – with me in attendance. Perhaps I would be in the newspapers one day – but as I hadn't yet been popped off the story probably wouldn't have enough appeal.

Coneetcha in later life.

All this brings us to the **morning of Friday 16th December** when the troops seemed to have gone to ground. Probably they were hunkered down to recover from the effects of having spent several hours chucking mortar bombs apparently haphazardly in all directions. It was not quiet for long. One contingent, hiding in the deep gutter of the road at the bottom of the hill, had settled just below us. Higher up, not far beyond our paddock, the opposing forces were entrenched along the hillside. We didn't know who either group was supporting, but they continually exchanged sporadic shells, some of which fell short and therefore landed amongst us. They made craters but, luckily, nobody was hit.

Somebody had brought a portable radio, a relative rarity in those days, so, bunched together in the field, sheltering close behind the Joys' house, we huddled as silently as possible to catch the crackling BBC. The announcements were not news to us since the broadcasters had been informed by the British Embassy in Addis, and they, in turn, were gleaning snippets from refugees like us, who were arriving from all directions. Embassy staff – Mr Joy, Mr Dickson, and others – courageously sallied out on reconnoitring forays in town among the frightening bullets; but we still had no news of the Jarys or of Princess Ruth and other members of the Imperial family.

Early on Friday 16th tiny 'planes dropped pamphlets round Addis saying that bombing would begin at 10am. All civilians were advised to clear out. Dishevelled and distraught people began to pour into our gymkhana field and, by midday, we had some 150 evacuees. John Tiffin extremely bravely drove right across town to inform the British Embassy that Commonwealth subjects in the Gulele district had taken shelter in the nearby Japanese Embassy where safety seekers were being well looked after. Then he made the long, dangerous drive back to be with his wife.

Amongst the arriving refugees we were relieved to greet Mr and Mrs Jary, bruised, very depressed and weary after a harrowing two days. First the Imperial children, who they loved as their own, had been forcibly removed; then they'd had to lie low under intense fire for 48 hours. Each time they'd tried to escape bombardments had forced them back, until a chance, brief, clearing of troops enabled them to make a dash. They tore out of the palace gates without personal harm but their car was badly damaged. The Jarys told us that events had taken members of the Imperial Bodyguard inside the grounds completely by surprise and they were shooting to protect the Emperor's home without knowing at all what was going on, or why, or who they were fighting. Mrs Jary was very shaken and distressed, but she rallied bravely. The Jary's little daschund, Minxie, was even more traumatised than her owners.

Gates of the Jubilee Palace.

Among the latest arrivals was a young Swedish couple whose adorable blue-eyed, pink-and-white baby girl, was born on December 12th, a few days before she'd been expected and two days before the *Coup* started. She spent her first days *under* her bed instead of *on* it and her parents were extremely relieved that she had not elected to arrive on schedule, which would have been right in the midst of the worst of the fighting.

All the refugees' consumable supplies were pooled and the various communities: British, South African, Canadian, Australian, etc. each elected a representative who co-ordinated arrangements and noted what food had been brought in by whom. I am not sure what purpose the list-making served except, perhaps, to keep us busy, and our minds off bullets and mortar bombs. I was put on the food committee. All available fresh stuff vanished in stew, mash and fruit salad for lunch. Alas! Rations were very short as we were advised not to break into our tinned supplies yet. By teatime the Embassy ladies had baked and there was cake for the children.

Karen spent the day lying on her face giving a humiliating exhibition of panic. Some of this was probably due to delayed shock but when I chivvied her she pulled herself together – so long as there was nobody around to see. Her behaviour angered and shamed me. In our field there were few adults without children. Their reason for concern was much greater than ours. It was up to the single folk to work for the community: prepare and cook meals, distribute blankets, allocate tents, list food that was brought in and decide how to spin it out to best advantage... and we had to keep calm not only as an example for the kids, but also to support each other.

The youngsters were a bonus and a menace. They had to be occupied. Organising games and songs, telling them stories, seeing who could find the most remains of bullets splatted against the trees in our wood, kept me from sitting down and thinking, which might have reduced me to a pulp of fear. It would have been all too easy to dissolve into terror; but all round (with few exceptions) panic was kept in check and stiff upper lips were fashionable.

In our paddock we acted as if we had become accustomed to the gunfire which clattered a constant background. Even the whee-ee-ee-ing of a close ricochet only caused eyebrows to be raised and just a few of the nearest people to fall flat! Small military planes now started to drone overhead. Bombs appeared to land haphazardly. New arrivals from town looked at the flimsy tents, listened to the overhead rumbling of planes and weapons, and wondered if they had fled from potential danger to merely a more exposed target.

By Friday evening the bombing seemed to be over and most people left – except for the occupants of six tents who lived in places where fighting was still in progress. During the day several young East African men, who were studying in Addis on an exchange system, arrived from the University in a minibus organised (with great difficulty) by Dick Greenfield, of the University. The students had passed the previous nerve-wracking night

H.I.M: Haile Selassie at a Red Cross Fair in earlier and happier times. A young Prince Paul is behind his right shoulder.

huddled in college rooms and were obviously hugely relieved to reach sanctuary – such as it was.

Public feeling was running high against Ethiopian undergraduates some of whom had demonstrated for Mengistu. The East African scholars didn't look in the least like Ethiopians, and they hadn't participated in the protest march, but they were scared stiff of being mistaken for those who *had* demonstrated. They clung to the Embassy and were extremely unwilling to move.

Showing great bravery Dr Matt, a devout Afro-American, Dean of the University, circulated constantly during the fighting, picking up the dead and succouring the wounded. In spite of his noble work, when feeling was running high against College students who it was thought had taken part in the protests, he was booed as he accomplished his humanitarian deeds. Needless to add that *he* had not participated in the demonstrations.

Mengistu had euphemistically called his supporters "The Crown Prince's Party". In fact it had been the Crown Prince, Asfaw Wassan, who, with his amateur radio equipment, had managed to beg the world for help, and had informed his father, the Emperor, that he himself (Asfaw Wassan) had been taken prisoner.

Dick Greenfield disappeared. He was missing for about a week and stories explaining his absence were innumerable: He'd been shot; He'd run away; He'd taken the ringleaders out of the country {How? – By road to Kenya? – To Eritrea? Both highly unlikely in view of the state of the so-called 'roads'}; He had gone to meet the arriving Emperor in Bishoftu – in fact the Emperor landed in Addis; and so on. Each story was wilder than the former. I saw Dick on New Year's Day just after he had supposedly 'come back to life'. He was excessively sunburnt and his hair was incredibly sun-bleached; but he wouldn't say where he'd been. One of those 'impossible' stories – or maybe even wilder adventures – had been true.

Maybe the well-built East African students were right to be petrified. By now the tide had turned. The Bodyguard, who had supported Mengistu's *Coup*, were on the run, with the Emperor's army after them, killing on sight – especially targeting big, strapping fellows. My servants, Zeleka and Waldi recounted later how, at this stage, a gang crashed into our garden hunting for escaping

Guardsmen. They fell upon Waldi. Because he was tall and sturdy they assumed that he was one of the Emperor's Guard and would have summarily dispatched him had Zeleka not screamed:

"Show your legs! Show them you have no puttee imprints!" (Puttees were part of the Imperial Guard's uniform. As they had to be tightly wound they left marks on the wearers' legs.)

Small and wiry, with a dark, screwed-up face, which was endearingly like that of my little Grivet monkey, Zeleka had no need to fear that he would be taken for an escaping member of the Imperial Guard. He was thus not frightened out of his wits; and he was no fool. Desperately trying to yank up his jodhpurs Waldi yelled again and again that he had no puttee marks on his legs. At this the trigger-happy invaders paused. There was a lot of jabbering. Of course it's impossible to pull the tight lower ends of jodhpurs up one's calves so Waldi had to strip while the gang stood around, obviously enjoying his fear and embarrassment, and eager to polish off their victim.

Cunningly, while Waldi was being menaced, Zeleka disappeared to the hidden corner of the stable where he and Waldi had buried a tin beneath a stone under a heap of tack. Sensibly he extracted only some of the emergency money that I had given them. The sum that he extended as a bribe to Waldi's torturers, together with photographs of Waldi with my animals, clinched the matter. The tormentors accepted reluctantly that he was a gardener, not a Guardsman, and clattered out of the property squabbling over how they would share the cash. It was fortunate for me that they hadn't penetrated into the house, but it had very nearly been 'curtains' for Waldi.

The Embassy couldn't order our movements; but that afternoon I was strongly advised not to return home. Major Bumpus had only just managed to rush past our house under a veritable storm of gunfire. Mr Joy and Mr Dickson, who had been patrolling town, also reported much firing in our region. Both had had to double out double quick from there! I abandoned hopes of getting home to boost the servants' morale and to remove some valuables because looting had been reported. I had also wanted to see how the Kenyan girls were getting on at school. Being boarders from outside Ethiopia, without homes to escape to, they wouldn't have been able to leave the dangerous locality.

By Friday evening most people had left our campsite. Trippers! The nursing sisters had been rushed back to the hospital in an embassy car flying a flag. By now we 'Permanent Fixtures' were camping in fine style. Luckily the weather was beautiful – with sunny days and cold nights, typical of December. Turning a deaf ear to bullets and mortar shells we could imagine that we were on a deluxe safari. We even had the use of a pair of taps that supplied hot and cold water. The East African students made an excellent camp kitchen and kept the fire supplied from a dead tree which Mr Peel had had chopped down for our use. I cooked us all a makeshift supper and two college lecturers who, like us, had not been allowed to return home, opened tins and did the washing up.

Before the 'trouble' people had been invited to cocktails with the ambassador and his wife. "On Friday December 16th to meet the Commonwealth Students" said the invitation. In truly British style, and as we were all on the compound anyway, the cocktail party was held. We washed and brushed up in our hosts' bathrooms and, then enjoyed civilised conversation, drinks and mésés. After that, down the hill we trotted, changed back into camping clothes, and proceeded with the supper described above.

Friday night, as on Thursday, started calmly except for bursts of shots now and again. As I pulled blankets round my ears, in the vain hope of blotting out sounds of warfare, I wondered if we'd still be under canvas on the next night – or would we be at home? – Or might some of our group be dead? Karen and Roy slept on the floor in the Joys' house but the rest of us decided we preferred our air mattresses and the relative privacy of tents. However, by 4.30am a pitched battle was in full swing north-south and east-west across the Embassy compound; and, unpleasantly close to us, a crazy, trigger-happy machine-gunner with no apparent target was firing in all directions. We would hear: "Rat-a-tat-a-tat-a-tat…" followed by a pause in which, distinctly, he threw out his empty rounds and put in new ammo. Then off it went again: "rat-a-tat-a rat-a tat-a-tat…pop! pop! POP!…" Three people stayed in the tents but, with the rest, I repaired to the Joys' floor. This was littered with refugees including the Dicksons (from their home lower down the Embassy hill) who considered, that having children, it was unwise to stay in a thin-walled house close to the road.

Coneetcha and Whiskers spent each night in my car, Whiskers nestling between Coneetcha's paws or crouching in the curve of her body. They made a delightful picture. I put the car in as sheltered a spot as I could find and covered them with a piece of old rug but every morning the blanket was on the floor. At the peak of the evacuation there were about five dogs taking political asylum but there was never more than one monkey.

To my relief both of my pets behaved admirably. Coneetcha thought it was all a grand picnic and enjoyed every second, having a great time with the children; while Whiskers held court all day to a changing audience of admiring youngsters and fascinated adults. As they were all very gentle with him he responded by being perfectly charming to one and all. He didn't bite anyone and only scratched a small girl slightly, and by accident, when he fell after missing his footing on a slippery car. Actually Whiskers was extremely alarmed by the shooting and was absolutely terrified by the planes which zoomed very low across the Embassy. I wondered what instinct told him that these noises spelled danger. The way he clung to me, chattering with fear, was very touching. In the following days, at home, he screamed in pathetic panic and dashed for cover every time one of those wretched planes passed overhead.

Saturday 17th **December** dawned bright and moderately free of bangs. Our little *ménage* of university lecturers, students, Karen and I revelled in a breakfast 'banquet' of grouty coffee, cornflakes with powdered milk, bread and jam. Neville (a coffee broker) joined us with a planter friend who was hoping for a coffee-growing job near Bonga. The latter was gent enough to praise my brew – despite his coffee expertise, and in spite of the grouts!

It was decided that, if we took care, we could visit our homes, make various observations in town and report details to the Residency upon our return. There was a woman lying awkwardly on our drive. I recognised the wife of the *toukul* dweller next door. She was known to be a bit of a toper so, under the circumstances, it was understandable that she had temporarily succumbed to one *tej* (Ethiopian mead) or *talla* (beer) too many. When Waldi opened the garden gates I inched the car past her rumpled body and asked angrily: "Why haven't you moved Asenavetch? Where is Kumsa, her husband? Tell him to take her away!"

"She's dead!" he replied flatly. "And her husband has gone mad. You can hear him now, screaming and screaming. He's attacking everybody. We are afraid to move Asenavetch's body without his permission. He's threatening even ghosts with his machete."
She'd been scared by troops searching the *toukuls*. As she fled, shrieking, they had put a shot through her shoulders.

When I asked my gardener/groom why he was wearing his best dark green jodhpurs and jacket while his usual outfit, plus a vest and a pair of underpants waved breezily on the washing line I was told about the fracas when Waldi had nearly been chopped and shot. "It was absolutely *essential* that he changed *all* his clothes," explained Zeleka without even a glimmer of a smile on his normally mischievous face. He was simply reporting on a shameful occurrence that had overtaken Waldi during an appalling and terrifying ordeal.

I praised the servants and helped to feed the animals, glad that they were still alive and in reasonable condition. Waldi and Zeleka were delighted to accept a heap of potatoes that I had bought from a roadside vendor – with borrowed money! When we heard the now-familiar rattle of sten guns passing outside our fence, Zeleka and I dashed behind the house but, to my amazement, Waldi continued mixing the horses' bran and oats. He didn't flinch or stop mixing. He just muttered: "*Zimbel! Bakka!*" (Shut up! Enough!)

Karen and a Norwegian friend turned up at our bungalow in his big car. We loaded it with a lot of stuff and they disappeared. I went on to visit the Kenyan girls at school. They were calm but frightened and wanted to be taken to the Embassy. There was no one with the authority to allow me to remove them so I searched through a veritable Back of Beyond of tortured alleys for the Indian Director. She had taken refuge in a quarter which made me think of stories I'd heard of insalubrious London before the Great Fire. Steep, narrow, streets twisted between overhanging, wooden houses. It was not easy driving over the deeply holed-and-rutted, mud road. A few shots were being potted off but it was no time to allow oneself to be worried by such a commonplace occurrence. As I cautiously bumped up the inclined, rocky, rubbish-cluttered lane a mass of civilians suddenly poured out of the houses and rushed towards my car, passing me with wild eyes. Saris and Ethiopian *shammas* trailed behind as they fled. Ahead, approaching, I saw a line of armed men. That was enough!

Never have I reversed so quickly or under such trying conditions!

Back at school, in view of the latest development, the Swedish Matron permitted me to remove the girls. With springs sagging I conveyed six pupils and a few of their possessions to the Embassy. How they all fitted into my car was a mystery. The Norwegian, with his big station wagon, was at the camp so he and I went back to school where we collected the remaining girls and more of their baggage. He very gallantly returned a second time to fetch their blankets. The lasses fitted smoothly into camp life, became part of our group of 'settlers' and helped very nicely with chores. In the evening one of the East African college students strummed a banjo while the rest of us sang and had a jolly little dance round the fire.

None of the 'Permanent Fixtures' could return home on **Saturday 17th** because of continuing battles round our homes; but by afternoon the rest of town was quiet enough for Karen and me, with four of the East African College students to be taken by the Military Attaché down to the Tsehai Hospital. The young men did a valiant job stretcher-bearing: carrying in victims as they arrived, and moving patients into and out of the operating theatre. On Sunday another four went down and they arranged a relay of teams to continue the work for as long as it was necessary.

Blood was urgently needed. Karen, who'd given blood before, laughed at my fears. (I was in an absolute blue funk!) Yet about this she must have been braver than about other matters because, having given her pint, she fainted 10 minutes later. Neville and the coffee planter gave blood too, but for half an hour I made swabs for the operating theatre. By then, having controlled my fears, I went down to give my pint; but – being plagued by recurrent malaria, and having only recently suffered such a bad bout that it had turned into Black Water Fever which nearly put an end to me, my offer was rejected. Boy! Was I relieved! Silly – but there it was! Deciding that when my malaria was no longer a problem I'd offer some blood in any case, I returned to swab making.

Planes started circling overhead and the town became filled with joyful, typically African ululations. The Emperor was returning! Happy people lined the streets and cluttered rooftops to catch a glimpse of their Lion of Judah. One of the hospital sisters dashed in. "Come on!" she urged. "Come and see!"

We tore down to the gate where we waited some time amid a wildly-cheering crowd, but we never saw the Emperor because finally, surrounded by tanks, armoured cars and many outriders, he very sensibly left the airport by an unusual route and, took up residence in the old Palace. It would have been impossible for him to return to the Jubilee Palace near our cottage where his nobles had been slaughtered and running battles carried on.

In the rush to greet the Emperor the coffee planter fell and broke his shoulder. As he himself said:
"What a darn stupid thing to do at a time like this!"

Would the Emperor's return precipitate war or bring peace? Once more the 'Permanent Fixtures', lacking permission to return home, convened in the Embassy field. Karen and Roy slept in the Joys' house but the rest of us, yarning in the paddock, were joined by new arrivals from regions where the situations had become tense.

When the general mopping up had been going on, panic-stricken Imperial Guardsmen tried to disappear into the woods and over mountains, including those behind the Gulele district – the area to which, with the best of intentions, I had evacuated Yeshi, Nigatua and their children! Many fleeing Guardsmen were hacked to pieces by the pursuing army, and probably personal feuds were settled in those days. For some time afterwards bodies, and bits of bodies, were found among the jet-black, long, vertical rocks formed by monster basalt crystals that cluttered a small gorge of the nearby river.

On their Gulele compound near the Pasteur Institute, William and Sheena were at home with their two young sons when shots, shouts and screams exploded from all round. Looking out of the window they saw men running desperately across spacious lawns. Behind the fugitives poured black silhouettes spraying machine gun bullets. William said he would never have imagined that so much fear could emanate from distant fleeing shapes. He and Sheena bundled the children under the table in the hall and started to barricade doors with chairs. When, in case he might need to defend his family, William hurried into the kitchen to find the biggest knife available, he was transfixed by the sight of a screaming man with his guts hanging out, rushing towards the family's home. There was a machete handle still emerging from the fellow's side. William was literally paralysed with shock: immobilised, but shaking as if he were suffering from a frightful case of Typhoid Fever. Sheena came through to discover why he was taking so long to find a weapon. She shrieked, pulled him into the hall and vomited. The worst aspect of it all, she said later, was seeing the injured man, who should have been thoroughly dead, hurtling away across lawns, screaming desperately, not trying to keep his dangling intestines in place, but holding his arms in a harp shape above his shoulders and waggling his hands as Ethiopian women did when they performed the weird Spirit Dance. Later the victim was found, dead and very gory, sprawled across the veranda of their neighbours' bungalow.

William and his family were in an extremely disturbed state of horror when they joined us in the paddock that Saturday evening. Every now and again Sheena and the children exploded into gulping sobs. I wondered why they had crossed town to reach the British Embassy and had not fled to the much closer Japanese Embassy; but they were in no state to answer such trivial questions. Their stories of the Gulele district made me worry about Yeshi, Nigatua and their babies. Had their inadequate *toukuls* protected them? Had they been victims of crossfire? Would Yeshi's little girl be traumatised for life by scenes such as those that would certainly scar Sheena's children?

Despite such worries, by now the 'Permanent Fixtures' were completely tuned in to firing. I was very proud of being able to explain to a newcomer what a mortar was, how it worked, and exactly what it sounded like! I could differentiate between noises of bren guns, sten guns, rifles, and grenades. For most of Saturday night neither bullets nor bombs came anywhere near us and, blasés about being under fire, we slept fairly peacefully in the paddock until, suddenly, such an intensive barrage broke out that we didn't even dare to run for cover. Scrambling under an Embassy truck which had a high clearance, we preferred not to admit how little protection it offered or to realise that if a bomb landed on the truck its fuel would explode in a fireball. As the cold night air seeped into me, I wondered whether it was really worth pressing my nose into a clump of coarse grass in order to be killed on 'British' territory rather than allow myself to be bombed in the comfort of my bed at home!

STINGS IN THE TAIL

And so to **Sunday morning, It was December 18th**. The ambassador and his wife went to church, and their prayers must have been answered for later the 'permanent fixtures' were allowed to return home. En route we noticed a lot of smashed walls, broken windows, corners off roofs, and such like… On the whole the ammunition used had been light so, in spite of the quantity that was popped off continuously for seventy-two hours, there was surprisingly little *serious* damage apart from round the Ministry of War where much destruction was evident, in Adowa Square where a murderous battle had taken place, and at the ammunition dump on the Bishoftu road, which had been the scene of ghastly events.

At our bungalow all was well, except that Kumsa, the husband of Asenavetch, the woman who had been shot, was still squatting on his doorstep howling mournfully and unceasingly; and Ollie, my eagle owl, had been smithereened into scattered feathers that now blew about the garden. Although a huge and splendid specimen he had been morose and vicious, accepting bits of rabbit and chicken while he recovered from a collision with a car. Once cured, he remained in our garden, superb but still surly. Frightened by the turmoil he must have flown up in confusion and attracted the attention of a trigger-happy soldier.
I grieved over his tragic demise, but was grateful that nothing worse had occurred.

Short of food, Waldi and Zeleka, who, incredibly, had decamped for only one night, had plundered our vegetable garden and eaten one of my rabbits. I was glad they had shown such initiative and begrudged them nothing. The house was several bullets the richer, embedded within the mud walls, and there was a small crater in the horses' field. Waldi was proud of a memento in the form of a section of tank which he had found outside our gate; and in the middle of all the hullabaloo two more chicks had hatched.

No sooner had we heaved a sigh of sad relief than loudspeaker cars circulated advising people to leave the district, as a big finishing-off effort was about to start. The contents of our cars were unloaded in record time and heaped untidily in the cottage. As Karen shot off hoping to reach Roy's place, I hurriedly stabled the horses and then made for the Post Office where I stood in a congested and disorderly telegram queue. The proposed cable to my parents: "Menagerie unscathed" did not take into account Ollie's murder but it was succinct and conveyed a comforting picture. In ninety minutes I progressed three yards towards the front of the queue, so, giving up, I joined Karen at Roy's house where, during lunch, we discovered that life round there was just as hot as it was at our bungalow.

Afterwards, reluctantly mustering all my patience, I trotted round to the Post Office again. In my bunch of eight cables that I was sending off for friends as well as for myself, were some that Mr Singer, the Austrian Consul, had asked me to dispatch so, on this attempt, I flourished the impressive stamps that embellished those official forms. On the strength of these I was attended to in half an hour; but one of Mr Singer's cables was addressed to Frankfurt and, saying that there were several 'Frankfurts', the official wouldn't accept that message. Telephones were reputedly working but I couldn't get through to the Austrian Consulate from a public call box and, when I tried to reach the Singers' house, I ran into firing. Removing myself as rapidly as possible I headed for the British Embassy. There it was assumed, correctly as it later transpired, that Mr Singer's telegram must be meant for the big Frankfurt in Germany. The telegram was given to the British Embassy's 'telegraph boy' and it got sent off.

By now it was evening and I was at home. I hadn't had time to return to help at the hospital; but a message was passed round to say that they were organised and had no more need of assistance. People 'phoned us to know if/how we had survived and everything was cheerful despite a lack of electricity.

When the background of intermittent shots became a tremendous barrage, Waldi and I dealt with the horses at high speed. My bedroom was on the side where the explosions were heaviest and most numerous so I pulled my mattress into the remotest corner of the dining room. Whiskers spent the night in my bed because his bedroom box under the roof of the stable was very exposed.

The firing continued to be heavy all night and, even though her room was more sheltered than the dining room, Karen crept through to curl up beside me. I was pretty scared myself but would never have dreamt of admitting it! I even thought nostalgically about the companionship experienced on the Embassy floors!

The next morning, Monday, I found that school would be closed till further notice so Zeleka and I spent the time cleaning, washing, and ironing – with the charcoal iron because the electricity was still off. Waldi was busy in the garden. At one point, when a squad went up the road firing steadily, I was amazed to see him still calmly cutting dead heads off plants. Thoroughly fed up with recent events he was, as before, muttering:

"Zimbel Bakka!"

You'd think he would have been more affected after the terrifying experience when rebels hunting for escaping militia on our property nearly shot him dead.

I discovered a machete under the cushions of the settee.

"Well," explained Zeleka, "one of us slept in your home and the other was in our quarters. We had to be ready to protect the houses and ourselves!"

Indeed. They had been extremely brave. They might have had to fight off looters or escaping guardsmen desperate for something to eat. Karen regained her aplomb and went visiting. She returned with friends for coffee; but no sooner had I set out the cups and got the water boiling, than she and her pals took off again, without having drunk or eaten anything. Arriving back an hour after our normal lunchtime, she ate, and then subsided amid total chaos in her room, and slept till evening. I assumed she was getting rid of a lot of delayed shock. None of us were acting entirely normally.

When all was practically straight I ventured out to visit the Hudsons, where I found a couple of University lecturers. The five of us chatted and played with our hosts' lovely little daughter. For a very brief interlude we felt happy to relax after all the tension of the past few days. But such illusions were soon dispelled.

As I started organising supper sporadic shooting started all over again. Like Waldi, I felt that it was high time all this nonsense ended and I was tired of being frightened. Zeleka was gamely waiting to help prepare the meal but his face had a strange pale-grey tinge that showed how terrified he was, and his hands shook so much that the plates rattled as he tried to lay the table. We had all of us had nearly more than we could take of close shooting.

42

I sent Zeleka into his quarters where he would probably be below the line of fire and also protected by our house, and devised a method for keeping Whiskers down on the floor of the hay room where I hoped he would be safe. His instinct was to leap from bough to bough so he naturally objected to being restrained at ground level. He screeched sounds like a miserable football rattle, stood on his 'tripod' made of hind legs and tail, and bounced furiously up and down. His eyes flashed deep garnet anger. Perhaps he wanted the company of his friends, the horses. Being constrained at floor level he would not benefit, as he usually did, from heat rising from their bodies. I put Coneetcha into the hay room to console him and, hardening my heart, I left him swearing shockingly in monkey language!

The barrage continued with fluctuating intensity and I wondered what on earth "they" could be firing at! My supper over, there was still no sign of Karen. I needed to keep busy in order to distract myself from the blood-curdling howls of Asenavetch's husband, who was still dementedly mourning his wife with ear-splitting screams. Hoarse yells were horrendous and creepy enough in daylight, but by night his ghoulish shrieks made my hackles rise.

As I hadn't yet baked my annual Christmas cake for the vicar I decided to try to do that. It would take my mind off events. A candle or paraffin lamp might have attracted the shooters' attention but plenty of starlight entered through the rear wall of the kitchen, which was all glass, so I was able to mix the ingredients for a fruit cake and fire up the gas oven.

Then I lay on my mattress in the dark dining room and worried about Karen who had not returned for our usual 7.30 supper. At 9 she 'phoned to say that she was at the Ras Bar and was intending to come home to eat soon. I advised her to stay away as heavy shooting was in progress all round; but she insisted that she would return before long. By 10pm the situation was deteriorating throughout our region and becoming extremely frightening. I was also weary of waiting for my lodger and terribly worried about her.

A bullet-splattering fellow had installed himself at the corner of our gate. I was afraid that the slightest movement would focus his wildly-flailing weapon into deadly action so I tried to contact Karen at the Ras, to advise her to keep away; but she had left. The 'phones of her particular friends weren't working. Squatting in the dark on the floor, using a dimmed torch to see the dial and keeping my head as low as possible, I called other places where she might have gone, but my efforts were in vain. Dreading what would happen if anyone arrived and disturbed the trigger-happy soldier I lay fearfully, on my mattress behind the dining table, which I had turned upon its side and dragged into my corner. I also pulled Karen's mattress and set it up vertically against the table as extra protection. Delicious smells were starting to emerge from the oven.

Kumsa's abysmal screeches began to grate dreadfully. They were spine-chilling wails like a dirge, yet they conveyed a sense of animal howls. Suddenly there was a more specific, even closer shot than the general background firing. It was followed by a clatter at the bathroom window that was always left partially open. Though small, a man could nonetheless squeeze through it. Was this some escapee who would bring reprisals upon our household? Had our shooter aimed at him? I froze into my mattress. Was the trespasser armed? I felt my hair standing on end. My eyes strained into the darkness. There was a thump which echoed through the house as the intruder landed on the bathroom floor. Together with the scrabbling there was a slight slither. A python? A large specimen had recently been seen near the school netball pitches so the sports area had been put out of bounds till the serpent had been caught and, having been displayed and admired, then released in a more suitable location. Was its mate now gliding across the floor towards me? My imagination went into terrified, melodramatic overdrive!

The scrabble-slither emerged from the bathroom and slowly crossed my bedroom. All the rooms of the house were interconnected and all the doors were open so I could distinctly hear the unwanted visitor's progress. My fevered mind imagined clinks – as of a chain. Thoughts of Scrooge's ghost tortured me. The intruder investigated my bed, and wardrobe… I stopped breathing!... Reaching the hall the noise paused, but soon it scratched across to the entrance of the living room. Now the foraging guardsman/python/ghost was really close. Should I get up and run? I sank as far as possible into my corner, my eyes popping out of my head, my limbs shaking.

The slither-clank, *hurtled* down the length of the dark living room, claws scraping on the floorboards. My end had surely come! It *scrambled* over the dining room table and landed heavily on my cringing chest! Whiskers! *How* had he escaped from the hay room? The shattered link at the end of the short length of chain that remained attached to his belt testified to the shot that had severed his light restraint. The chances of a bullet reaching the hay room, penetrating its wall, skidding along the floor and then finding a link in Whiskers' thin chain must have been infinitesimal. He was lucky that it hadn't arrived a yard closer to him! Was Coneetcha dead? unharmed? lying wounded? I didn't dare go outside to investigate, and was consumed with anxiety and guilt for not going to her aid; but it would have been suicide. The barrage of shots was intense and randomly directed.

Whiskers must have bolted instinctively for safety into the house, though he might well have scooted for the big trees in the Crown Prince's gardens, and that would have meant tragedy. He was quaking and needing a lot of comforting. He knew about the bathroom window because, in happier times, it had been his greatest disobedient delight to scramble in through that window, bite the toothpaste tube, and with his naughty little black hands and feet, smear the contents all over floors and walls. It always amazed me how far an enterprising monkey could spread a little toothpaste.

Smoke started to seep round the house and the cake smelt decidedly overdone; but I didn't *dare* move into the kitchen because a group of excited men had started marching to and fro along the road, shouting and firing rifles into the air. Presumably they were only celebrating victory but, obviously inebriated, they were firing wildly. Automatically comforting Whiskers, I hoped that the cake wouldn't catch fire!

From next door the ghoulish moans and shrieks of Asenavetch's deranged husband became increasingly unbearable, till, abruptly, there was another particularly close shot and his lamentations were cut off in mid-scream. He had been sent to join his wife! The ensuing temporary dead silence was as eerie as the previous noise had been terrifying; but it gave me enough courage to wriggle on my tummy into the kitchen and turn off the oven. The cake might not be edible but at least it would not set fire to the daub and wattle house.

Exhausted as much by the terror that Whiskers had transmitted to me as by all that had happened, I must have finally fallen asleep for, at midnight, Karen woke me by hooting her klaxon to ask me to unbar the gate and let her in. I was not keen to venture outside and make a noise, which might attract unwanted attention; but, after a dopey moment, I was sufficiently awake to realise that our shooter at the gate was silent – presumably departed – or dead.

DAY OF FUNERALS

The next morning, **Tuesday 20th,** Karen rose late and immediately went out. Various friends 'phoned and were horrified to hear that I was on my own. They insisted that I should go and stay with them; but events had demoralised me and I decided to stay where I was. I was especially shaken and depressed when a great many groups of mourners keened their ways past the house carrying loosely-wrapped bodies that wobbled on shoulder-high, stretcher-like biers of slatted wood. Some of the weeping people threw ashes upon their heads. They abandoned all attempts at control and wailed tremendously. It was excessively morbid and depressing.

Not only common folk were involved with death. The massacred noblemen were buried. To honour them the entire Diplomatic Corps congregated at the end of our road. Their cars shuffled about – presumably until they were in the correct order of protocol – and then, at last, flags fluttering, they drove off very slowly. As they passed our bungalow in a long, impressive and tragic file, I happened to be at the gate, negotiating with a vegetable vendor. The British Ambassador waved and smiled at me. Most unsuitable – but I greatly appreciated the kind and re-assuring gesture.

Instigators of the *Coup* either committed suicide when surrounded or were strung up at choice spots around Addis. Public hanging, a great deterrent to crime, was practised in Ethiopia. It was considered very suitable for a priest to take boys from his congregation to watch a criminal on the back of a lorry having a rope placed round his neck and left jerking and dangling from a gibbet

46

when the truck drove away. Some years previously I had accidentally come upon just such a revolting event. Having no wish to repeat the horrifying experience, I avoided the hanging sites for several days till it was safe to assume that limp bodies would have been taken down and removed.

AND A FINAL SURPRISE...

Two unexploded bombs beside the school gave us an extra day off work until they were harmlessly defused. After that the shooting died down.

Karen decided that she could no longer live near palaces.

I went with three friends on an adventurous, bandit-dodging trip through awesome scenery to discover a route up the highest mountain in Ethiopia, {The account of that incredible, amazing trip is the next story in this book.} On my return the Christmas holidays were over.
The *Coup d'Etat* became just a nasty memory.

My parents in Cyprus asked a visiting Queen's Messenger, who had been at the British Embassy during the *Coup*, if he had seen me and how I had been coping. He admitted with embarrassment that he had seen several young women but didn't know if I had been one of them.
"She probably had a monkey with her," suggested my father hopefully.
"Oh *yes!*" replied the diplomat immediately. "I saw *her*. And she had a dog too".
That put me in my proper place: noted only because of my pets!

As far as I was concerned, some time later, there was one last result of the *Coup*. I was invited to lunch at the British Ambassador's house. I arrived nearly late and a trifle dishevelled thinking that I had been asked to make up numbers. To my *horror* I discovered that

47

there were about twenty diners and I was the guest of honour! Although totally dumbfounded, I think I managed to maintain the requisite flow of polite conversation with the Ambassador on my left and the dignitary on my right. I didn't drop a fish knife or strawberry spoon; and the lackey behind my chair never had to pick up my table napkin. I wondered why I had received such an unexpected tribute until a murmur reached me that it was in recognition of my efforts in evacuating the Kenyan girls and for organising people/children/ meals in the Embassy's Paddock Camp. Amazing!

****

The Emperor was deposed in 1975 and died in grisly circumstances.
****

Grölle and me – with Whiskers 'off-stage'. Skal is hiding as usual!
Ethiopian horses were small but strong. Grölle was a powerful jumper who loved taking part in gymkhanas; but he adored thumpy music. If the band was playing when we had to do our round, or when we should have been competing in a bending race or other event, he would start to 'dance', and nothing could stop him. I didn't appreciate his wonderful leaps and prances but they were very entertaining for the watchers in the stands. I used to beg the bandmaster not to play when Grölle and I were participating.

Open charcoal iron on a stand. The charcoal has been
fanned to make the charcoal flame a bit.

****

CLIMBING RAS DASHAN, THE HIGHEST MOUNTAIN IN ETHIOPIA.

Christmas holiday January 1961:

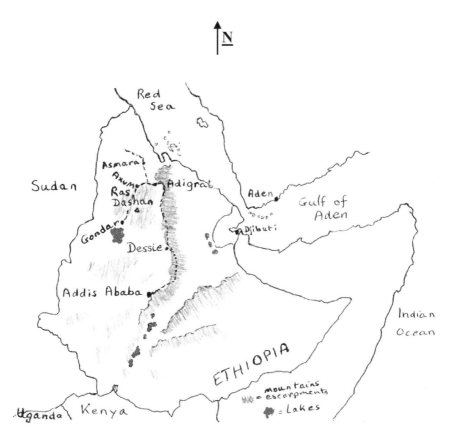

PREAMBLE

From Addis Ababa, the capital of Ethiopia, to reach Debarraque, the starting village for the walk to Ras Dashan, we spent 4 days driving some 600 miles counter clockwise through immense isolation and sensational mountains. Had a road going in the opposite direction existed we could have made an appreciably shorter journey travelling the other way – through equally magnificent scenery.

Never before or since have I ever been on a more scatter-brained and badly-prepared expedition than the one to Ras Dashan.

The holiday fell into four parts:
A   Getting to Debarraque. (4 days)
B   The walk to and back from the mountain. (6 days)
C   One day for a brief visit to the fabulous town of Gondar with its wonderful, historic buildings. That is not detailed in this holiday diary since it will be covered in another book: "*Completing the Circuit*", which describes a journey I made the next year with a female friend driving from Gondar to Addis. We had to construct the road and contrive bridges as we went along.
D   The return from Debarraque to Addis Ababa. (4 days)

In this account the homeward drive has been mentioned only briefly since, apart from three extra events, most of it was simply a reversal of the outward journey.

1ft = 30.48 cm = 0.3048m   1000 ft = 304.80 m   8000ft = 2438.4 m

Height of Ras Dashan : 14,930 ft a.s.l. (4,550 m)
Height of Mont Blanc 4810 m.
These days I start puffing above about 8,000ft a.s.l.
The altitude of Addis lay between 8,000 and 10,000ft a.s.l. so in those days we were well acclimatised to high places with little oxygen. Hence we were very lucky because on the walk the altitude scarcely affected us.

(*Shifta* = notorious bandits with a world-wide reputation for cruelty.
Dejasmatch = nobleman)

PART ONE: DRIVING TO DEBARRAQUE

1

WAS IT SENSIBLE TO GO?

When invited to join the Lockewoods' expedition through northeast Ethiopia, I felt honoured. I never suspected how *ad hoc* their adventurous arrangements were and didn't know how lucky they'd been in the past to escape violent or agonising death at the hands of men or Nature. I learnt the hard way. They didn't *want* company but they needed companions to help defray costs. Maybe I was asked to join the expedition because few others had agreed to risk it.

Before our departure, among a group of friends who had gathered to play tennis, Neville voiced disapproval.

"I wouldn't venture on even a day picnic with the Lockewoods, let alone go on a long journey though wild, fearfully-desolate, *shifta*-infested regions."

"But," I bleated, "they've explored so many fantastic, exotic places !"

"Yes. They're very intrepid explorers of Ethiopia. I grant you *that*. Adrian's taken wonderful photos of untamed places and savage people; and I particularly remember his stunning shots of horrendous sulphur lakes 125m *below* sea level in the volcanic eastern territory."

"I was quite petrified by his dramatic pictures of unsavoury tribesmen," put in Clara, Neville's tennis partner.

"Ha!" leered Gustaf, "Especially the portraits of those dreaded Danakil, eh? ... Whose young men aren't qualified to marry until they've got a string of dried human testicles round their necks."

Clara shuddered.

"They've been everywhere; but they're terribly disorganised and irresponsible."

"You'll end up in some *Dejasmatch*'s dungeon."

"Or as the main course of one of their raw meat binges."

I tried to make my retort dignified and scornful:

"Ethiopians eat strips of raw meat cut from living *cattle* not slices of humans!"

Neville shrugged and twirled his tennis racket.

"Call!" he invited me, and thrust his racket towards Clara.

"Smooth" I chose.

"It's rough," said Clara.

Was that an omen? Was I in for a bumpy time on the trip with the Lockewoods?

Not only were they apparently unreliable, but also the final throes of the 1960 bloody attempt to depose Haile Selassie was only just ending. Serious rumours of Civil War were rampant. Should I heed my friends' warnings and stay in Addis? What a terrible waste of two week's holiday! I was young and unrealistic. Anyway, on the trip and totally out of contact with civilisation, we wouldn't even *know* if Civil War erupted; so I packed my gear, and, by arrangement, on Thursday 5th January, skived off school when my pupils were still doing their last end-of-term exam. Their answer papers would be collected by a colleague and left at my bungalow pending my return. Other papers, for marking, came with me.

I was shaken to learn that, due to fears of the impending Civil War, (and perhaps because of our Leaders' reputation for scatterbrained stupidity) three of the original seven members of the expedition had cried off. Apart from reducing our complement of strong men from 5 to 2, this also meant that we would have just one, instead of two, Land Rovers. The incredibly bad state of roads (when they actually existed) and the total lack of facilities in the wild and inhospitable countryside in those days are difficult to convey, or even imagine, in our present epoch of comfortable travel. It was always wiser to have a duplicate vehicle when going on trips. They could pull each other out of swamps or sand. Only one set of spare parts was needed. If the worst came to the worst, travellers could cannibalise and contrive one functioning vehicle in which to reach home. Spare parts? Special tools? While on the Ras Dashan trip I realised with horror that the Lockewoods never bothered to carry either. It was then too late to do anything about it!

I was even more devastated to hear that, instead of leaving their infant daughter with friends in Addis, as planned, Mrs Lockewood had decided to take her with us!

"But,Thérèse!" I wailed. "There will be no clean water – maybe no water at all... No shops... No doctors... Marthe is only 18 months old. She can't climb cliffs and sleep on ice shelves..."

Thérèse was unmoved. "We'll find a village from which to start walking and we'll leave Marthe there, with Turuwerk, our maid."

I gasped. However good-natured the maid might be, she was completely uneducated and definitely not used to European standards. A couple of days into the journey I realised that she was also extremely stupid. Poor girl! She probably had no idea of what she was in for.

I exchanged shocked glances with Callum, the remaining (fourth) insane teacher about to set out on this trip, but we said nothing more. Like me, Callum was in his early twenties. The Lockewoods were a strange couple, come late to parenthood. We assumed that, being older, they must be more experienced and wiser than we were. Thérèse threw into her car an unwrapped bundle of nappies. Turuwerk would wash soiled diapers in any suitable stream that happened to be in our vicinity

"What if Marthe falls ill? Malaria! Diarrhoea! There won't be even a primitive clinic for hundreds of miles..."

I was seriously worried about the baby. In 1960-61 we hadn't even heard of jars of baby food or of factory-made baby-carriers.

"What if a rabid dog runs raging round the village? – or a mad goat or mule?"

Rabies was rife all over the country so this was not an unlikely eventuality.

"Which village do you plan to leave them in?"

Adrian waved a remarkably empty map. Surveys of Ethiopia started in 1968 so, in January 1961, we didn't expect detailed information about far-flung parts. Travellers relied on hand-drawn charts provided by friends. These gave directions such as:

'After a burnt hovel drive 4 miles on gravel to a collection of woodpiles, then turn right onto a cut-up dirt track. In about 5 minutes you'll come to a ford which can be used if it hasn't rained recently. Cross the river. Head downstream towards a baboon-shaped rock... "

"We're not quite sure of the mountain's exact name so we don't know where we'll start walking," said Adrian, folding the blank map. "I haven't found anyone who knows the district, but that's not surprising since it seems that no-one has explored that region. We'll start asking questions when we're in roughly the right area."

Callum and I, squashed into the small cab of Adrian's extra-short Land Rover, exchanged glances and hoped for the best. Less than six years ago, using mules, Thomas Pakenham, helped by the Governor of Gondar and accompanied by local grandees, plus a party of twelve armed soldiers, and numerous porters, had been the first white man to explore an area south east of Gondar. He caused a stir amid archaeological and historical circles by stumbling upon an unrecorded medieval church, and antique documents. He also located a precipitous mountain on which ancient emperors had sequestered their male relatives. Now, unaided and with neither official support nor a posse of guards, our party of only four were hoping to achieve a much longer journey on foot through the equally wild, mountainous and unexplored region just north-east of Pakenham's exploits.

2

OFF THE ROOF OF AFRICA

Adrian, Callum and I left Addis in the cranky Land Rover followed by Thérèse driving a poky, low-slung, sports VW Ghia. A more unsuitable vehicle could hardly have been selected for the ridged and potholed gravel roads; and its passengers were Marthe, a vulnerable baby, and the moronic maid. Moreover the Lockewoods forgot that by taking the Ghia, the baby and the maid, they would entail unplanned expenses. So for the last few days of the holiday we counted even *cents* ultra carefully and freewheeled down hairpin bends on horrendous escarpments to save petrol.

"Shouldn't Thérèse go ahead," asked Callum, "so that we can help if she gets a puncture or something?"

Adrian just grunted. He disapproved of "Madame", as he called his daughter, being brought along. He was cross, not because he was worried about *her* safety, but because she would be a nuisance.

We had scarcely emerged onto the main road when the Land Rover packed up. Callum and I were horrified, but Adrian crashed open his door, saying:

56

"Oh! I forgot! Stay there."

He lifted the bonnet, heavy with the worn-thin spare tyre, performed some adjustment, and returned, wiping his hands on his shorts. Then, looking satisfied, he restarted the vehicle and we were off. During the next 15 days this little pantomime was repeated often but we never discovered what taciturn Adrian touched so magically. He knew his car and had learnt from experience how to deal with its eccentricities.

Starting on a reasonably good, loose-gravel road we headed east, veering later to north east, across huge expanses of empty, rolling plains. They were covered in swishing gold and pale green vegetation, with here and there an attractive rocky outcrop where Aloes and Red Hot Pokers were starting to glow. Due to the high altitude the air was clean and clear, colours were vivid, and the sky the usual, amazing, deep blue. (Exposed to high levels of UV, and knowing nothing about anti-sunburn creams we were a well-tanned lot.) Clumps of Eucalyptus indicated rare villages, which, near Addis consisted of thatched, circular mud huts, picturesquely fringed with Banana trees. Horses, mules, donkeys, cows, goats and sheep grazed round the hovels. Chickens fussed, and dogs lay about scratching.

A laden donkey approaches a village.

As we gradually gained altitude the dwellings became thick stone structures, solidly built against the cold climate and icy winds. Here crops and Eucalyptus trees had vanished and the primitive huts were starkly surrounded only by weather-breaking rock walls. Signs of life decreased but a few goats, browsing on foliage that sprouted from rooftops, gazed superciliously as we passed.

At lunchtime the terrain changed abruptly as a tremendous escarpment suddenly appeared beside us. It dropped vertiginously eastwards. We had reached the edge of the main Ethiopian plateau which is five times the area of England and Wales combined. Its undulations range from 2000m to more than 3000m above sea level.

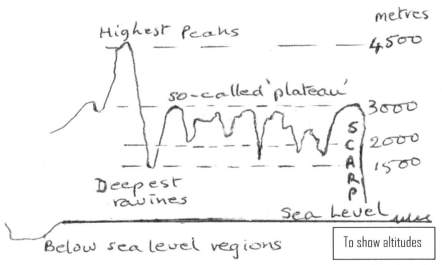

Summits poke higher, to more than 4550m. Very few of the deeply-etched ravines plunge below 1500m. For many centuries Ethiopia's daunting, precipitous edges isolated its colossal mountains from any neighbours or travellers. This, the largest continuous high-altitude region in the continent, is called "The Roof of Africa".

We stopped where, between looming promontories, the Termaber Gap sliced vertically through the scarp's sheer cliffs. Dramatically framed by this cleft, we could distinguish the small village of Debra Sina, 2438 dizzying metres below: a different world, miniaturised by distance, with hotter temperatures, other plants, distinct crops, changed houses, unknown tribes… Callum gasped and, with a questioning look, pointed at my school altimeter – which I had illegally borrowed for the trip.

"We've climbed well over 900m from Addis," I told him. "It says we're now over 3600m high." {cf The highest point in the Pyrenees which is 3350m a. s. l. The top of Ben Nevis is 1345m a.s.l.}

The Termager Gap.

Callum, Adrian and I explored round the gap to threatening barks from a mob of Gelada Baboons which are known as 'bleeding heart baboons' because of the shocking, bare, red patch on each chest. This gives them a fearsome appearance. Unused to intruders invading their territory, they objected to our presence. Geladas are found only in Ethiopia where they live in vast, high-altitude meadowlands, and are the most terrestrial of mammals after Man.

"There you are, Callum," said Adrian indicating their long, luxuriant coats. "Get one of those magnificent manes to wear on your head and you'll be accepted as a very brave fighter."

"I thought Ethiopian warriors wore *lion* manes."

"They do. But if you live in the high mountains you're not likely to meet the king; so you prove your valour by killing a huge Gelada instead. They're known to be terribly ferocious although they eat only grass and roots."

"Thanks a lot!" Callum gazed at the fierce-looking creatures with awe.

"Just look at those fangs!"

"At least the brutes aren't cold."

Though warmly wrapped, we were nevertheless shivering in bitter winds that whistled down the breach. By the time the Ghia finally appeared, 75 minutes later, I was anxious as well as frozen. Marthe had been car sick and fractious. Thérèse, unused to driving outside town, was traumatised by skids. Throughout the trip she was exhausted every evening and I could only admire her guts for plugging on day after day. Marthe sometimes slept in Turuwerk's arms but often she must have been a sore trial, wriggling about,

Man wearing a Gelada mane

59

bored, difficult to manage, demanding more amusement than could be supplied in the Ghia's confined cockpit.

Glad to move on from the Termaber Gap, (in those days called The Mussolini Gap) we nursed the cars a further kilometre, and 50m higher, to a magnificent tunnel. The vehicles pinked painfully because their engines were tuned to Addis conditions which held more oxygen. We had eaten a slice of bread and cheese before leaving but I was now hungry and expected to picnic beside the monument at the far end of the passageway. There we would be shielded from the biting wind, with the immensity of the Horn of Africa displayed at our feet. Had we been capable of seeing beyond countless overlapping and gradually descending ridges, we'd have observed a varied panorama and, eventually, the Red Sea.

The vastness of Ethiopia has an impact that surpasses imagination. It's probably the most spectacular and breath-taking of Africa's many remarkable territories. At the time of our Ras Dashan expedition, it was still wild, savage, and peopled by a diversity of primitive, often hostile, tribes. We were heading across the north east of this barbaric scenery, where, during their (1935 – 1941) occupation of what was then called Abyssinia, the Italians constructed a superbly-engineered gravel road from Addis Ababa to Asmara, in Eritrea. Through huge empty regions this amazing route coiled up cliffs, zigzagged over gigantic mountains, scratched across sweating valleys and crawled over unbelievably endless plateaux. It had only three branches. Two, going right, went down, through desert, to Assab and to Massawa (both on the Red Sea). Between those, another branch, going left, reached Gondar via incredible gorges and precipices.

During the more than 20 years that had passed since its construction this remarkable highway was surprisingly well-maintained by American aid but, inevitably, sections developed ruts, potholes and terrible corrugations that caused spectacular spins. Bandits (the notorious *Shifta*) made some sections of the countryside, and especially the road, life-threatening. Felling thorn trees, they erected barriers to halt vehicles which they then appropriated. Travellers – if lucky – were left naked by the roadside. The less fortunate lost their lives as well as their trucks and goods. Driving only by day, a percentage of lorries *did* get through the awesome scenery and frightening conditions, but in the early sixties very few private cars ventured over those dirt 'highways'.

We four expatriate teachers, working in Ethiopian schools, lived in Addis which, at heights of between 8000 and 10000 ft (2743 – 3048 m) a.s.l., straggled over the side of the impressive Entoto Range. The altitude had doubtless affected our brains adversely for, like a miniscule dot labouring across infinity, we proposed to spend our Christmas holiday travelling along this formidable ribbon of bad gravel. Our aim was to locate, if possible, and try to climb, Ras Dashan, the highest mountain in rugged Ethiopia and the tenth highest in Africa. We must have been deranged.

Exit of the tunnel - where I had imagined we would have a picnic.

3

A SOJOURN IN PARADISE

As we emerged from the tunnel an apparently endless expanse of mountains opened up eastward for hundreds of mauve-tinged miles. There was no mention of food. I knew that Callum was missing his lunch, too, for, as we left the elevated "Roof of Africa" and curled down the far side of the escarpment, his tummy rumbled emphatically, and not just because of the truly breath-taking drive.

61

The spellbinding view and terrifying drops provoked an awed silence in the Land Rover as our stony road coiled over great supporting bulwarks and twisted down, and down, and still further down. Looking back we could see, against the massive grey curve of one of the higher bastions, the word: DUX. This impressive sign, referring to Mussolini, had been built into the wall in *vast*, white stones by the Italian engineers.

Two of the bends. Here the road went *through* the bastion as well as over it.

It would have been wise to spend the night in Debra Sina, the first of two tiny villages in this region; but Adrian was not satisfied with our progress and we paused there only long enough to take fuel. As the petrol server pumped his lever backwards and forwards bright yellow liquid frothed up into adjacent, transparent, glass cylinders. Marthe was excited by the gushing brilliance as golden bubbles sank from one drum into the tank of the car and more froth swirled up the second container. It was a long-drawn-out process so, for something to do, I tried pumping. But it was hard work which, cruelly, I left to Callum and the petrol 'boy'.

In the middle of a curve some distance beyond Debra Sina the Ghia choked to a stop. Every time a vehicle broke down my heart froze. Luckily the Land Rover was not far ahead so we noticed the halt and, in strained silence, our driver turned back. Then, as Adrian

fiddled under the Ghia's bonnet, Callum and I hovered, waiting to help if needed. When the sports car was again mobile perhaps we should have driven back to Debra Sina where we might possibly have located a mechanic and some sort of parts that we could have adapted; but Adrian looked at the setting sun and, with a muttered:
"We're not yet in *Shifta* country," he headed on towards the mini-hamlet of Komboltcha.

Every evening after dark, baboons of all types would be asleep, curled along ledges and in crannies among the rocks; but we regularly saw pairs of yellow and green orbs reflected in the headlights. The lowest probably belonged to mongooses and genet cats. Civets and jackals were taller, and the highest of all the reflections came from leopard or hyena retinas. The latter sometimes roamed in packs and produced a constellation of twinkles. We tried to see the shadowy shapes of creatures behind the eyes, and occasionally we would hear spine-chilling hyena whoops. All this was entertaining and quite normal. The same happened regularly round Addis when we went out after dark. The carrion eaters made an excellent job of clearing away all garbage and, if sometimes they also cleaned up a drunken sleeper, – well – then that was unfortunate – but probably didn't cause much sorrow.

Komboltcha Traffic jam (cows and people).

In thick darkness, at 19.45, we stopped in Komboltcha at the misnamed *Albergo Paradiso*. With two garrulous Italian truck drivers we sat on benches at a plank table to dine off unadorned pasta and leathery omelette. Outside the *Albergo*'s back door the transporters' 'boys' cooked their own meal on three stones over a fire. In blistering sunshine, or cowering in freezing high-altitude storms, these assistants spent their days perched atop the lorries' teetering loads, eyes scanning the mountains for possible indications of *Shifta*. At night they slept in the cabs of their lorries.

We expected Turuwerk to eat with us but (wise girl!) she didn't fancy the food of Paradise! Clutching a small cylindrical bundle wrapped in brightly patterned material, she sidled in and isolated herself on a stool at the far end of our plank table. When I had carried luggage from the Ghia into the '*Paradiso*' this whiffy bundle had felt like a lump of sponge rubber, wider in the centre and tapering at its ends. As the maid undid the cloth its contents bounced open to expose a springy circle of what looked like the solidified top of bubbling, brown porridge. It was the size of a small tray. This was *injera,* the staple diet of Ethiopians. It's made from flour of highly nutritious *tef,* a millet which has very small seeds. A gruel-like batter of *tef* is poured onto a flat, circular griddle. Bubbles form and burst as the batter sets into a thick, round, spongy "pancake". Spicy relishes,

called *wat,* are placed on the "pancake", parts of which are torn off, folded round the spices and popped into the mouth without touching the lips which would get burnt by the spices. To our European eyes Turuwerk's supper looked rather like brown crêpe bandage, but in fact *injera* and *wat* make delicious eating.

The picture shows one of the beautiful 'basket-tables', made of very finely woven, dyed grasses, that were used to serve and to transport layers of *injera.* The layers were placed on the tray-like table-top below a removable lid. Portions of various sauces were placed on the 'crêpe' – convenient for dipping into them the torn-off pieces of *injera*.

When a load of injera was being carried from A to B it was easiest to place the bottom of the table over the bearer's head as shown in this drawing of Injera going places.

Lid

table

That evening the maid had no sauce. Soon she slipped outside where she was obviously happier sitting on a stone, sharing the 'boys'' fire – their only source of light – and accepting some of their stew to eat with her 'crêpe bandage'.

Our 'rooms' were small cells separated by plywood partitions that reached no higher than head level. In mine, hoping to discourage bed bugs, I discarded a thin kapok mattress onto the mud floor. Over the bed of very knobbly, split Eucalyptus branches went the waterproof sheet that, when trekking in bad weather, I normally wrapped round my tent, and onto this I placed my air mattress and then my sleeping bag.

The echo-y, barn-like establishment had no ceiling. Small scurrying sounds – no doubt of foraging rodents and/or snakes – came from the rafters that supported the corrugated iron roof. From the grubby mud outside the back door a thin metal pipe, like some painful plant, emerged vertically. At its top 'bloomed' a tap that spat a weak, horizontal spray in which anyone inclined to cleanliness could perform public ablutions.

After supper, by the light of a paraffin lamp, Adrian wrote his diary and I marked exam papers. Soon I had the lamp to myself. The lorry drivers were first class snorers!

65

In the way of infants Marthe woke very early, opening her mouth and eyes simultaneously. Her piercing prattle echoed round our 'rooms' and, even though Thérèse carried her out to Turuwerk, who had spent a cold night in the Ghia, we were, by then, all awake.

Only Callum had been bitten. He bared his waist to reveal a line of nasty red bumps left by a hungry insect.

"Bah!" said one of the lorry drivers, who came to join the inspection committee. He prodded Callum's afflicted tummy disparagingly.

"Bah! Only – Basta – how you say? – a – fleas – Orl O.K. Yoo-a orl O.K." He implied that we were lucky to have escaped the attention of bugs, and slapped Callum's hand away from the bites.

"Non gratare!" he ordered, and then went to place his face hopefully in front of the horizontal tap.

There had been no recent cases of typhus so we presumed that Callum's flea had not been infected. If the bites had come from bed bugs we'd have had to attempt the almost impossible and terribly tedious task of fumigating Callum's luggage. By the end of the trip we would probably have all been infested. It was therefore a relief to

be able to agree with the lorry driver about the fleabites. Callum spread his sleeping bag over nearby rocks in the pale, chilly sunlight and we partook of bitter coffee and equally harsh, compact, grey bread. The landlord, wearing the universal jodhpurs and tunic, placed a catering-sized tin of delicious South African apricot jam on the table. Had we known how long we'd have to survive on that breakfast we might have managed to swallow more of the gritty tack.

Magnificent Aloes and huge Cacti trees flamed all along our route

4

KOMBOLTCHA TO QUIHA

Despite protests from Callum and me, the Land Rover set off from 'Paradise' ahead of the Ghia. Shortly after leaving Komboltcha we saw the turn-off that went right: eastwards, down through scorched deserts and past sheets of white crystalline salt lakes, to the Red Sea Port of Assab. Our own route continued northward towards Asmara in Eritrea. Even though there were no road signs it would have been difficult to get lost. Here we were at the first split in the road since Addis. All we had to do was take the first left here and then, at the next fork – nearly 400 miles ahead – choose left again and, from there, continue for roughly a further 200 switchback miles where we were not bothered by any side roads.

For nearly three more days, at altitudes that varied between 1500m and 2500m a.s.l. we struggling doggedly up, and down, round, and over, huge expanses of "just Africa". The Great Scarp, western edge of the Rift Valley, was a tremendous wall on our left. The other side of the Rift was on the far side of the Red Sea. Sometimes we climbed, crossing cold, eroded regions along the Scarp's flanks. Sometimes we dropped to sweltering plains at its feet. The scenery was stunning, the isolation amazing. On our entire journey (there and back) we saw only ten private cars – in the 'towns'. So far, between Addis and Komboltcha, there had been occasional lorries serving the Assab-Addis trade, but after Komboltcha the traffic, if such it could be called, dwindled to almost nothing. Occasionally we saw a small collection of native huts, or a patch of cultivation, but the sum of hamlets that we passed along the entire journey, amounted to fewer than the number of Marthe's little pink fingers. We would have noticed more agriculture had it not been the dry season when crops had already been collected. But in January even dry stalks had been stacked as fuel or animal fodder.

We climbed steadily to Dessie (2500m a.s.l.), a tiny town, and the capital of Wollo Province. 250miles from Addis, it was the seat of Asfaw Wassen, the Crown Prince. For years my father had discussed (in an advisory capacity) Current Affairs and World Finances with His Imperial Highness. They became friends, and, when I was a teenager, my family were guests of the Crown Prince and his wife in Dessie for one sumptuous, luxurious weekend. The manful efforts of my brothers (aged about 6 and 8) to play in the splendid gardens with the tiny girls (then probably 4 and 5) and their younger brother were hampered by the Imperial children's extreme shyness and the close attendance of their nurses. At parties the two little princesses were resplendent in candy-floss-pink, organdie dresses with full, standing-out skirts which emphasised skinny, black arms and legs. They wore fashionably big bows in their hair.

On this trip to Ras Dashan we didn't presume to call at the palace but humbly took petrol, and had a puncture repaired. Then we grundled on – down to a vast area of glutinous black soil where the land was dotted with row after row of cotton plants.

Someone had warned us that this trip would consist of one huge mountain massif after another, with unbelievably vast plateaux between the ranges. This prophecy was fulfilled to a T. Unending hours of grinding painfully along on poor springs, and in clouds of dust, could have caused frightful boredom: but there was always a fantastic crag, or magnificent Aloes, or amazing hairpin bends... to provoke gasps. Grandiose scenery and the way the road went on... and on... and on... kept renewing a sense of great wonder. There were

Fisherman in a reed 'boat'.

also two very pretty blue lakes to admire. Lake Haik has an island on which, in typical Ethiopian manner, there was a circular monastery with an ostrich egg at the central apex of its thatched roof. With incredible skill the locals balanced on, and managed to spear fish from, improbable craft made from bundles of reeds. (On Lake Tana the local boatmen used the bundles as planks to make small canoes.)

At 2pm, famished and tired, we stopped the Land Rover at the head of the immense Alamata Valley. Behind us descended spectacular miles and miles of tortuous curves, and then a gigantic plain stretched apparently endlessly south. There were Prickly Pear bushes, Aloes, Acacias, 2-metre-high thistle plants, and many boulders, but apart from soaring birds we saw no motion anywhere. Where were Thérèse and her passengers?

The Lockewoods had organised provisions and Adrian lugubriously informed Callum and me that we had no lunch since all the food was in the Ghia. It seemed strange that such a large item should have been wedged into that cramped car and also that no thought had been made to share so vital an item between vehicles. The grandeur all round couldn't numb our gnawing craving for sustenance. Hungrily we devoured chocolate and biscuits exhumed from my pack. Later, under his seat, the temperature of tepid tea, Adrian discovered a couple of small bottles of lemonade, which fizzed over violently when opened. I was appalled that we carried so little to drink. The most basic preparation on any trip was always to carry ample supplies of water, not only for human consumption but also in case of a holed radiator.

Plain after plain between range after range ... going on ... and on... for ever.

(Warning! There are 4 bits of doggerel in this book. Below is the first effort. If 'poetry' isn't to your taste just skip the rhymes.)

THE ROAD   goes   On...   and...   on...   and...   on...

As your Land Rover struggles 3000 miles from south to north up the length of Africa each current bit of track seems to extend on and on for ever; yet overall, the road has boundless variety.

The road –
　　　　like a carelessly
　　　　　　　　cast down string,
　　　　　　　　　　　looped
　　　　　　　　　　　　　mazed
　　　　　　　　　　　　　　　and twisted

　　　　　　　　　　　　　　　　in
　　　　　　　　　　　　　the
　　　　　　　　　　　　glaring
　　　　　　　　　　heat .

Coil upon coil
　　　　　　slith'ring
　　　　　　　　　down
　　　　　　　　　　　steep
　　　　　　　　　　　　　escarpments.

　　　　　　　　　　　　　peaks.
　　　　　　　　　　　sharp
　　　　　　　　　　to
　　　　　　　　up
　　　　　　creeping
　　　　　bend
　　　after
　Bend

Red,　　silver,
　　　　white, and yellow.
　　　　　　　On, and still onward
　　　　　　　　　　with miles flanked

　　　　　　　　　　　　　by scrub and Acacia.
　　　　over
Bouncing　　boulders.
　　　　　　Splashing through the streams.
　　　　　　　　　Marshes, palms and birds.

　　　　　　　Crocodiles and water snakes.

　　　　　Ferries non-existent
Bridges almost gone.
Then :-

70

Braving the Sahara.   Bedu silhouettes.
                              Sometimes flat, eroded...
                                        stretching straight for days.

Peaks that poke,

              and wadis deep.

                    Colours that amaze.

                          Crust that breaks, and stops you

                                        DEAD..............

                              skies.
                   to   the   Grey grit,
          streaming   brown grit..
     red dust,
White dust ,

                                                    Teeth,

                                        and hair,

                          and eyes.

              Finger nails to match too,

                              fully fashion-wise!

Vistas and views.
              Valleys and plains
                    Hamlets and emptiness.
                              Valleys and crags.

Massifs with castles.

          Mirages.

          Snow!

              The roar of the lion.

                          The shriek of the eagle.

     And still it grinds on   o'er the land with no end.

71

That evening, by rummaging, I located the food box – *in the Land Rover*! On subsequent days I would crawl over the junk in the back of the car while we were bumping along to excavate food and drink, and often I stayed comfortably sprawled over the bundles. It was a relief to stretch after sitting between the two men where my legs had to curl awkwardly round the vehicle's gearbox hump. There was no question of enormous Callum ever wedging into the middle, and Adrian was the driver.

Normally on trips, my friends and I had a strict routine: everyone took turns at driving, whoever's car we were using. The driver was permitted to ask to swap after one hour and *had* to give place to someone else after 2 hours. It was unwise for one person to drive to exhaustion and, besides, it was sometimes very boring being a passenger for hours on end. This system worked well, yet on this trip Adrian never suggested that anyone relieved him, which was probably just as well for neither Callum nor I could have nursed the tricky vehicle as he did. But his long hours at the wheel worried me. We relieved the bone-rattling hours with song. Luckily there was nobody to hear us!

At the head of Alamata we waited, and waited, for Thérèse to appear. Callum and I threw stones at rocks. Adrian, a renowned photographer, spent the time trying to figure out (in vain) why my recently-bought, second-hand camera wouldn't focus properly. A lorry arrived over the crest from the north and its driver, glad to see friendly humans, stopped to chat and to check that we were not stranded. Those Italian gentlemen of the road were incredible. They urged vehicles, which, though not the modern day juggernauts, were nevertheless pretty huge, round painfully looped mountain routes in a manner nothing short of miraculous. Of course, with their multiple wheels, they churned up the gravel, especially when they had to 'to-and-fro' repeatedly to negotiate bends. Many people whose vehicles, overcome by the dreadful conditions, had apparently given up the ghost, owed their lives to the truck drivers who knew tricks to get cars moving. If Italian magic failed, they attached the recalcitrant vehicle to the back of the wagon and towed desperate travellers to safety.

I once experienced that sort of assistance. It was *terrifying*!
The car, on the end of a dubious rope, pendulum-ed from side to side.

till we, its passengers, were certain we were about to career over the edge of a fearsome escarpment, or bash into a roadside boulder. Desperately hooting the horn (if it was still working) or flashing lights (ditto) was useless. The driver, deafened by his rattling transport, never heard or noticed, and his assistant on top of the piled goods, just assumed that we were hooting with joy, and waved cheerily back. Forgetful of the towed car, speedy Umberto, happily singing operatic arias in his cab, would rush along, over terrible corrugations, without stopping till there was an accident or till he reached a settlement where he could leave his devastated victims, grateful for his help and even more grateful for being released.

Our talkative friend agreed that it was the height of foolishness to leave Thérèse in the rear.

"Yoo go-a for the end-a" he ordered, shaking an admonishing finger at Adrian as he finally clambered back into his truck, left us in what seemed like endless infinity, and drove on.

By 4.15pm, when Thérèse eventually arrived at the top of the spectacular Alamata valley, we were heartily tired of magnificent views. Marthe had again been sick. They had stopped for an hour over lunch and to rest. Turuwerk looked exhausted and Thérèse grimaced with a tired face. No wonder! She was not used to long days of difficult driving with, moreover, a whining infant who wriggled about in a very confined space.

Champing at the bit, before starting the Land Rover engine, our leader allowed us just enough time to wolf three bananas off a bunch that Thérèse had bought from a street vendor in Kombolcha. As even Adrian had become worried enough to heed the Italian's advice, we ground forward in altered formation.

On tight hairpin bends up the breath-taking Amba Alagi cliffs, we circled at one stage, the edge of a terrifying promontory from which, in 1941, the Italian Duke of Aosta, preferred to jump into the abyss rather than surrender to the British. A mini-climate produced unexpected bright green patches of grass that glowed on tiny flat steps jutting below us from the side of the escarpment. Then it was down again, to cross desiccated fields in the Mai Chow valley, and on, and on... Reaching the little settlement of Enda Medhani Alem at sunset we should have camped. But not a bit of it! Ignoring the oft-repeated warnings of our finger-wagging friend, *Shifta* or no

Shifta, Adrian pressed on. The cars pinked yet again at the high Toccelli Pass but eventually we lumbered down into Quiha. Never had I been so relieved to stop.

"Well, we've escaped the bandits so far," said Callum wearily, scratching his waist. Pushing his hand away from his bites, hastily I crossed my fingers. Why did he tempt fate?

<u>5</u>

<u>FEASTS, VULTURES, AXUMITE STRUCTURES</u>

At Quiha we found a "marvellous" *Touring Hotel*. 'Marvellous', of course, was a comparative term; but after the *Albergo Paradiso* we felt we should have brought our evening dresses and black ties. We discovered properly separated bedrooms, beds with metal springs, and basins each with one tap from which there was actually a trickle of dubiously-coloured water. Turuwerk and Marthe retired immediately. The rest of us found the dining room clean; and the menu boasted fruit (at extra cost) as well as the usual pasta and chicken or 'rosta' (for which one had to be equipped with shark's teeth.). After our scanty lunch we ate heartily and it all tasted terrific! Then, as on the previous evening, Adrian scribbled in his diary and I marked exam papers; but it was so late, and the paraffin lamp so temperamental, that we soon gave up.

Before the others appeared the next morning, (Saturday 7th January), I went for a tour of the small village. Its one, rutted and stony, main street was lined with typical rectangular, flat-roofed Tigrean houses made of thin, horizontal slabs of stone. Some had an upper storey. Many had steps up to the roof so that goats and sheep could be kept up on the flat top, safe from 2- and 4-footed night-time predators by blocking the steps with a massive bundle of thorny branches. Between the slabs, from walls and roofs, sprouted tufts of withered plants that had flourished during the Rainy Season.

January 7th is the Coptic Christmas Day so on a slope beside the hamlet a slaughtered ox was being dissected for a feast. Crows and ravens, eagerly awaiting their part of the orgy, cawed a tremendous cacophony as they hopped boldly about the killing area. Round the corpse was a circle of woven trays, banana leaves and stretches of material – as many as the men who were wielding big knives. Each of these 'dishes' represented a family which had shared in paying for the slaughtered beast; and each family had to receive an identical portion. The heart, tail, kidneys, lungs, femur… everything – was chopped meticulously into 12 – 14 – 16 parts, (as many bits as there were families) and one sliver was dropped onto every 'dish'. Small boys, each in charge of his family heap, chased off daring all-black, powerful ravens, slightly smaller pied crows and many flies.

A few dots, circling far above, showed that vultures were already preparing to plummet into the scene. Later they sat hunched on surrounding boulders but the careful dissectors of the carcases had ensured that there was virtually nothing left for scavengers be they vultures, crows, ravens or the hyenas and jackals that would sniff around after dark. Only red-soaked earth told of the event.

A busy group of friendly but bloodied anti-*Shifta* 'policemen' was distinguished by their 'badge of office': tattered ex-army greatcoats. They offered cheerful greetings, but the gory sights didn't please me so I left them to their precise divisions of liver, lights etc...

An earthenware coffee pot, a small 3-legged Ethiopian stool and – vital accessory – my petrol funnel with a fine mesh filter which we should have had with us.

Just a few feet outside her front door, in the main 'street', which was like a stony farm track, a woman was pouring a spiral of *tef* batter from an old oil tin onto a big, circular, flat, metal dish. She was making *injera* over a dung fire that smouldered within a hole in the road. A delicious smell of Ethiopian coffee wafted from an earthenware pot in the embers. Any connoisseur would have gone into raptures over the elegant curves of the container with its cheeky spout and beautiful handle. Decorative patterns round the vessel's neck and belly had been incised into the clay. {Coffee derives its name from Ethiopia's south west district of Kaffa where the beans were first used.}

The lady thought I was a great joke and called her neighbours to share the spectacle. They were very affable, offering me coffee and *injera*, which, luckily, I was able to refuse without offending them, and showing me the dark, simple interiors of their houses.
"Why are the windows so high, and small?"
They seemed amazed that I should ask about such a basic matter.
"To stop the *Shifta* from shooting in, of course."
The roof of heavy stones covered with soil was equally defensive. Thatch could have been set on fire.

Laughing and prodding, the women stretched skinny arms to touch my flesh and to feel the texture of my cotton skirt, which was utterly different from that of their coarse, self-spun, self-woven, garments. Their clothes, which had no shape but which were just gathered loosely at the shoulders hung down to their bare toes.

The episode was entertaining and informative but they didn't talk the bastard version of Italian that was usually understood all over the country, and I found it hard to figure out their lingo that seemed to be a variety of Amharic (the language spoken in Addis) strongly influenced by a queer (to me) variety of Arabic. I discovered later that their dialect was probably related to the ancient scriptural language of Ghe'ez that had originally arrived from Saudi Arabia some centuries previously and which was still used in the Ethiopian church. Be that as it may, we managed to make animated conversation well enough, and when words failed gestures came in useful. In the doggerel on the next page:
The constables were an anti-*Shifta* patrol based in Quiha. *Talla* is a kind of beer, and *tej* is mead.
Entirely black ravens (powerful birds with massive beaks) are meat-eaters and scavengers.
African crows (also carrion eaters) are smaller with white napes and less-forceful beaks.

76

Christmas Dinner for the Quihans

On that Christmas day at Quiha crows and ravens squawked aloud
as the valiant village constables trooped eastward, in a crowd...
crossing scrubland, wide and arid, which the dawning sun washed red –
silhouettes – like ants advancing: khaki crawling; constant tread.
Waving knives, machetes, rusty saws, they chanted all the way
for the villagers had bought a bull to celebrate the day.

They were bent on killing cattle for a feast of warm, raw meat,
so the sombre birds were cawing for some leavings they could eat.
Distant mountains formed a backdrop, mauve and wrinkled, poking high.
Hordes of hungry vultures circled in the vastness of the sky.

Gallant Tesfaye, with his rifle, dealt the ox a felling blow.
Then the cunning butcher, Phanto, brought the gushing crimson flow.
Skilfully they skinned it. Jackals slyly gathered round;
till the great dismembered body lay in pieces on the ground.

There were fifteen homes to share it, hence each organ, muscle... there
was dissected to that number, so that all could have fair share.
Gory fingers cut and sorted ev'ry tasty bit of beast
such as femur, tail and ears... all divided for the feast.
Even horns and hoofs and eyes... the scrawny hide's rough, matted hair...
An identical selection for each household made with care.

Then, when all had been accomplished, bits of bones were gleaming white.
Fifteen plantain 'plates' presented dripping piles: a grisly sight.
Folk were happy. One dark pool of blood, soaked grimly in the ground
was unheeded by the soldiers as they set off homeward-bound.
Leaving nothing for the scavengers: the vultures, ravens, crows –
naught for jackals or hyenas – and forgetting all their woes,
they rushed, whooping, back to Quiha, where thick *talla* and sweet *tej*
frothed in monster pots of clay upon each doorstep's handy edge.

Twelve days later, on our return trip, the Quihans were again celebrating. This time it was the Feast of the Epiphany. In the dark hours after midnight, elders within the church started an eerie, haunting, monotonous wailing accompanied by sonorous throbbing

of large drums. These were long and heavy, with one wide end, which boomed a deep sound, and one narrow skin, which gave out a higher-pitched note. They were hung round the necks of young Servers and thumped by both hands – one palm at each end. The chief priest balanced a rectangular stone on his head. Carefully kept from view under an ornate headcloth, this represented the Arc of the Covenant, (i.e. Commandments given by God to Moses) and was the most sacred and precious possession of the church.

At dawn, apparelled in gorgeous velvets, and shaded by large velour umbrellas borne by altar boys, the clerics processed three times round the church and then, passing the sites where cows had been slaughtered twelve days before, they proceeded slowly up the hillside to a sacred spring. Robes and umbrellas of magnificent, glittering colours and liberally decorated with sequins, made a vibrant splash against the drab, dry mountainside. Wearing their best *shammas* over jodhpurs, or dresses, the village populace followed in a noisy gaggle.

The ceremony was protracted for hours as the priests took turns to read from the holy book and, with their acolytes, danced dignified measures, known as the 'Dance of David'. The stately steps were accompanied all the time by resonant drumbeats, strange singing, and clinking hisses of silver rattles, onomatopoeically called *systra*.

A priest's silver systrum. >>

78

A single pair of wire-rimmed spectacles was passed from 'reader' to 'reader' and nobody noticed that often the scriptures were held upside down when the celebrants 'read' aloud.

Villagers formed a long queue to immerse themselves, fully-dressed, in a pool where the clergy blessed them as re-affirmation of their previous baptism. Those of a more animist turn made offerings to tree, water and boulder spirits by pouring libations of coffee over the roots of a giant fig tree that grew beside the pool, and attached small rags to its branches. Some worshippers carried typical Ethiopian table-baskets holding food. These were tightly wrapped in gaudy cloths. Later, men competed on ponies by galloping about throwing sticks and spears at each other. Chanting women danced in tightly packed circles making their breasts bounce in the celebrated, special Ethiopian way by jogging shoulders abruptly up and down.

This painting shows Timkat (Epiphany) being celebrated.
Women vibrate their breast vertically. Warriors in animal skins are ready to cast spears. Richly-garbed clerics surround the chief priest, who has the Arc of the Covenant stone on his head. One drum (bottom left) is for the dancers and a different drum accompanies the priests' chants. People crowd round the church. Only clergy are allowed inside. I bought this painting from an itinerant artist in Addis but the writing mentions the Duke of Gondar's presence in this scene.

However, as I wandered round Quiha that early morning, Epiphany was still twelve days ahead and while Quihans were busy carving up their Christmas cattle I found my fellow travellers addressing the usual coffee, dark bread and huge tin of South African jam: plum this time, and still scrumptious, but not quite as delectable, we decided, as the Komboltcha *apricot* version. Then leaving unsatisfied vultures on their boulders, and the villagers to their raw meat, we squeezed into our vehicles and faced the lonely gravel strip that stretched grey and apparently endlessly across an awesome immensity of 'just empty Africa'. We saw a lot of that on this trip; and for hours at a time, apart from crows and the occasional indistinguishable blur (probably of rat or mongoose) that sped across the road, we spotted no living creature (man or beast).

We hoped to reach Axum – legendary home of the Queen of Sheba – that evening. If she existed, this beautiful lady, who charmed Solomon and thus started the dynastic line of Ethiopian Emperors, must actually have reigned in Southern Arabia. Her people crossed the Red Sea, and during the first 10 centuries AD, they ruled varying areas of Southern Arabia and great stretches of what are now North-East Ethiopia and Eritrea.

They brought with them an architectural style in which buildings were made from thin, horizontal slabs of stone, and built rectangular instead of the now more recent circular structures. Horizontal wooden layers and rafters of Axumite buildings had end timbers which protruded from the walls. When churches were, in later centuries, excavated from solid blocks of mountainside, the rock was carved to appear as if the ends of

In this sketch, typical Axumite-type, thin, horizontal stones, enclose a *double* keyhole window. The ends of poles which support internal structure protrude from the wall.

wooden beams were sticking out from the walls. Thus subsequent edifices, although entirely made of rock, aped the stone and tree-trunk buildings of previous builders. Axumite architecture also displays ornately carved keyhole-shaped windows, reminiscent of ancient Arabia.

That Saturday 7th, still at *relatively* low altitudes, skirting the uppermost plateau of Ethiopia, we travelled through a huge section of Africa which was dotted with historical venues. These were not only of the Sheban kingdoms. Here, in 1541 Portuguese troops, under Christopher da Gama (son of Vasco) fought and defeated Moslems who were then ruling the region.

In 1868, at Magdala, the British overcame the ferocious army of Emperor Theodore, an extraordinarily complex megalomaniac, who was brave, tactful, courteous, a formidable natural warrior, and eventually, deranged. He united great swathes of the country, in which, responding to teachings of British missionaries, he abolished slavery, reformed the tax system and introduced the novel idea of paying his troops instead of allowing them to live off plunder! Unfortunately a letter which he wrote to Queen Victoria never received a reply so, taking umbrage, Theodore imprisoned the missionaries and, years later, as he became increasingly demented, the emissary who was sent out to negotiate on behalf of the incarcerated evangelists, was alternately entertained lavishly and locked up. Defeated at Magdala, (by the British finally avenging the suffering pastors) Theodore committed a grisly and sad suicide.

In 1896 Emperor Menelik ll slaughtered 5000 invading Italians and their allies at Adowa. But these ancient battlegrounds, other historic sites, and mysterious *amba*-top monasteries were hidden among the mountains away from the road so we plugged on towards Axum, conscious only of the immensity and apparent emptiness of the terrain.

Drinking Grivet monkey.

6

QUIHA TO POST AXUM

So – Axum-bound, crossing unbelievable expanses of plateaux, we bumped along the ruts and corrugations of the amazing highway north from Quiha. A series of oddly-shaped, blue-mauve mountains, resembling unlikely stage scenery, suddenly popped up, one after the other, on the left horizon in the far and middle distances. They were the famous Simien Mountains and our objective, Ras Dashan, was hiding somewhere amongst those rearing summits. Their strangeness made me feel that I was dreaming.

An *amba* – less sheer than many.   Reaching the plateau is an act of faith.

Today we crossed a region of "*ambas*": tall, impossibly steep-sided mountains, with flat tops. Black and hard, some are the remains of long-dead volcanoes. All are geological anomalies left sticking up from surrounding plains when, over many millennia, the high plateau has gradually eroded. Monasteries perch on some of these summits though it's difficult to imagine how anyone could possibly climb to the tops, let alone carry up materials to construct buildings. A visitor has to negotiate vertiginous, vertical cracks or be pulled up a cliff by a thong of fibre or leather twisted together by the monks. If the rope breaks – tough! That clearly means that you are a sinner and not fit to enter the monastery. (Suggestion: Peak at the picture on page 132.)

Ancient Emperors stopped uprisings by incarcerating their male relatives on *amba* tops which made impregnable prisons. When the need arose the next ruler would be summoned from the natural isolated platform currently being used as a jail. I wondered how fit to govern the extracted ex-prisoner would be. On the way home we hoped to investigate one of these strongholds.

Spotting an Axumite-style church by the roadside we stopped to admire, and to wander round the precincts. A group of phonoliths was suspended from branches of a strong tree. These oddly shaped, but carefully selected, pieces of volcanic rock are struck by a smaller stone to emit bell-like notes. Candelabra Euphorbia stood immensely tall in a grove round the building. Together with Aloes and Red-hot Pokers these Cactus trees lined parts of our route, and were now heavy with incipient crimson and yellow buds. Later, when we lumbered home, the plants were all in tremendous bloom, and their brilliant flowers were a dazzling sight against ultramarine high-altitude skies.

Men, who we met later, by the roadside near Debarraque.

Many lonely miles beyond Quiha we passed through the next village, Adigrat, and soon after that we went left at the second of just two (!) turnings along the whole of the great northern highway between Addis and just before Asmara. Now we were driving roughly west. Some 100 or so miles further north beyond Adigrat lay the capital of Eritrea which Thérèse and I hoped to detour to on the way back; but we had to abandon our hopes of seeing Asmara as, on our homeward journey, money was far too limited to permit such giddy projects!

We found the Ghia beside the road. Thérèse complained that it was making extraordinary noises and steering strangely. My heart froze – as usual. This isolated spot, in *Shifta* territory moreover, was not a place to break down. Turuwerk was almost prostrated with terror and the rest of us looked around fearfully while Adrian again wriggled under the engine. With many grunts and smothered curses, ordering us to pass him various basic tools, he managed a 'repair'.
"It won't last long" he grumbled. "You'll have to drive carefully."
We breathed again – temporarily. Sensing the tension Marthe, of course, created merry hell and I was selfishly glad not to be travelling with her.

If it been Adrian's car that had given trouble we'd have been less worried. There would have been a fair chance of literally "finding" spare parts. At the time Land Rovers were just about the only vehicles that could cope with Ethiopian district roads but even *they* ocasionally did come to grief. Then their carcases were left adorning villages, or even sometimes abandoned beside country tracks. Desperate drivers could be saved by cannibalising these wrecks.

We lunched and sunbathed, overlooking splendid ravines and mountains, and reached Axum, supposedly the Queen of Sheba's home, by early evening. Nowadays it's a tourist destination; but in January 1961 it was a squalid, beggar-ridden village of narrow, winding, cratered, unevenly cobbled alleys full of litter and filth.

We sought fuel down these insalubrious lanes and, having, with difficulty, found a shack that stocked a weird-looking fluid, which was said to act as petrol, we bought it by the tinful, pouring it into the cars with some trepidation since it was liberally laced with floating particles and – need I say it – the Lockewoods didn't have a funnel with a filter, something that I would never have left Addis without. Why had Callum and I taken them so much on trust? Why had we never suggested a pre-trip meeting? (Pic of funnel on page 75.)

The "petrol" vendor also did a trade in antiques. He offered us a variety of silver items, including ancient-looking coins. They could well have been genuine because relics of past civilisations become exposed after every rainy season. The locals, who hardly ever saw unknown travellers, hadn't yet learnt the value of tricking strangers with false 'genuine antiques, sir'; but as none of us were numismatists, and as the coins were battered almost beyond recognition we didn't buy.

In the dust outside a disreputable mud hut lay a confused heap of two ancient, dismembered Land Rovers, a mutilated van and other unrecognisable bits of numerous vehicles. This was pointed out to be the Axum Garage. Adrian hunted among the various car cadavers and found a piece that could be adapted to improve his earlier repair. The garage man had a hard tussle to liberate this from its parent ruin and sold it to us at an inflated price.

I discovered a local souk (small, native, general store) stocked with the usual paraffin, bolts of material, matches, sacks of maize, bags of tef, a bicycle – very second hand – flip flops, head scarves in screaming colours, blankets, primus prickers, oil lamps and such-like treasures. It also had a small stock of tinned food so I made purchases to supplement the contents of the provisions box, which I had discovered to be sadly lacking in supplies.

In spite of the petrol trauma, the dirt, the beggars and the flies I was glad to fulfil an old ambition to visit still-sacred Axum, where Ethiopian kings, until Menelik ll, had been crowned. Vertical in a dusty uneven 'square' was one large, now well-known, granite obelisk decorated with a rising series of horizontal strips. Symbolic doors and windows were carved on the front face between these bands. The nine layers represented storeys climbing towards heaven. Beside this big stele stood, or lay, smaller un-carved versions, as well as several great fragments of a much more massive (34m long, 110 storeys) fallen monument with the familiar Axumite demarcations on *four* sides. All the monoliths had the same rectangular cross-section crowned with a semi-circular 'sky', or sun /moon emblem. The sadly neglected steles were all lying within a small area in front of the

Three Axum steles.

enclosure of the pretty, main church but they have since been re-erected, and their once-grubby precincts have become fine gardens. The church, surrounded by the ever-present Aloe bushes and Euphorbia trees, was of course, built in the ancient style, and women were not allowed in its compound. To console me, a dubious-seeming, and definitely unwashed, 'priest' invited me to visit the nearby small temple and also the 'church of Mary'; but these buildings were not in the Axumite style and I didn't want to delay the others so, despite his emphatic urgings with an elegantly carved metal cross, I didn't accept the offer and disappointed his hopes of receiving a cash reward. Nor, as time was limited, did we look for stepped buildings and deeply dug tombs of long-dead kings which were reputedly in the neighbourhood.

The priest, however, was not dashed by my apparent lack of interest. With what was perhaps meant to be a conspiratorial leer he waved his cross towards a middle-aged man sitting disconsolately on the steps of the main church.

"*Shifta*," he said.

What? Had I heard correctly? That respectable-looking fellow wrapped in a *shamma*...? He bore no resemblance to my conception of an authentic, swashbuckling, bandit. Perhaps "Introduce you to a real live *Shifta*, ma'am?" was the latest enterprising form of extracting cash from the tourist. So I smiled and went on my way; but my doubts angered the priest. He collared a passing youth and huffily ordered him to explain in English.

"He – very bad thieving – escaping from police. Church refuging. No house. No food. Must be begging. Go nowhere."

The brigand, having been caught in *flagrante delicto* during a raid, had then escaped from his captors and sought sanctuary in church grounds. The populace would seize him if he left, partly because they feared *Shifta* but mainly for the reward that might be given for his corpse. I turned back to look at the fellow with more interest. He seemed utterly harmless. I suppose that in the end bribes from his accomplices would effect his escape.

In those days, under the brow of a parched, brown knoll, there was a rectangular reservoir resembling an immense, muddy swimming pool. It had been hacked out of the hillside so was not visible until we climbed to its lip. Then a biblical prospect suddenly appeared. Down one end there was a graceful spread of long, shallow, beaten-earth steps that descended into opaque water. Opposite those steps, at the far end of the pool, the ground sloped to allow animals to drink. One side of the little brown lake was terraced upwards from the pond going in big steps up the mountainside. The other long side rose vertically from the surface, and then, having contained the water, it turned downhill.

At the Axum pool.

Women, in the usual shapeless-yet-graceful drapes, mud-coloured from washes in this water tank, were filling enormous earthenware jars and helping each other to lift these horrendous weights onto their friends' backs. Donkeys, horses, cows, swimming and washing humans, all availed themselves of the water. The people and conditions were all filthy and horribly unhygienic; yet the scene

87

was picturesque, and even pleasing, as everything was bathed in the lovely hues of a dramatically setting sun.

We were now definitely into authenticated *Shifta* territory. A few lorries operating between Assab/Asmara and Gondar passed through Axum, and these tempted bandits. So we really should have stayed at the mucky hovel that called itself the Axum Hotel, or camped in the dirt beside the obelisks. But whether in the 'hotel' or in our tents, the cars would probably have been broken into by these desperately poor people, and, had we camped, it would have been unpleasant to be constantly watched by all the eyes of the village while trying to keep the corresponding hands off our possessions. So we pressed on, passing some small, plain, tooth-like 'standing stones', left by pre-Axumite people.

Lit by a blood-red sunset of great splendour, we spotted a copse which would hide the cars, and bounced carefully across-country to establish a concealed camp beside a fearsomely cold stream.

"Are you going to fix the Ghia, Adrian?"

"No. It's too dark. Beside we don't want to attract attention by making more noise than we absolutely have to. We'll tackle that tomorrow."

We rolled a few large stones to form a shelter to protect the fire from the breeze and to stop its light from being seen.

But we'd been observed. Three sombre characters loomed  ominously in terrifying silence out of the darkness. They squatted close to us in a row of mute, threatening, black silhouettes, sticks poking skywards above their shoulders. Other mysterious objects bulged from below their cloaks – rifles? After customary greetings, there was a pregnant silence in which we did our best to ignore them. Then they announced that they were our guests. Oh Yeah!?

Suspicious young Axumite water carrier.

7

COLD CAMP, TORRID TAKKAZE

Trying to ignore our unwanted and scary visitors we started to pitch camp. Callum delved about in the back of the Land Rover.

"Has anyone seen my tent? I shoved it in behind the passenger seat; but it seems to have vanished."

"Oh, yes!" said Thérèse over her shoulder as she extricated a saucepan. "I took it out before we left Addis. We didn't have room for three tents."

The shocked silence was almost palpable. Callum couldn't sleep outside. There were roaming hyenas and jackals – quite apart from thieving humans; and it was extremely cold because, although we had descended appreciably, we were still at 2162m above sea level.

"But…"

"You'll have to share with Daphne. I expect there'll be room."

My horror soared exponentially. In the gloom as much as I could see of Callum's face made it plain that his feelings were identical to mine. She might have consulted us! I was speechless with anger. But there was no alternative. Luckily my tent could accommodate three (thin) people lying side by side; but what if I had brought a little pup tent, such as the one I acquired six months later? In that there was barely room for me to lie down, and it didn't do to try to turn over. Besides, Callum and I had met for the first time only three days ago.

But there was nothing for it.

"Sorry" muttered Callum. I was dumb. We set up our air mattresses at the extreme sides of the tent leaving as large a gap as possible between us; and when we turned in we lay on our sides with our backs to each other, both of us very embarrassed and furious with Thérèse.

As we heated water, our intimidating audience inched still closer. A frightened, prickly feeling shivered down my back. Callum bristled but was restrained from action. We gave our 'visitors' bread and tea, and they seemed more or less satisfied. Maybe, seeing the Lockewoods' extraordinary sleeping arrangements, they decided that our goods were not worth robbing. The eccentric tent was adorned with strange bits of wire, that stuck out in all directions, and were a danger to eyes, but which didn't attach to anywhere in particular. In the face of the unforgiving hardness of Ethiopian terrain, 'normal' tent pegs, pathetic aluminium skewers that sink obediently into soft European soil at pressure from a shod foot, here simply bent and ended as useless coils. I solved this problem by using ten-inch steel nails and these I hammered into the concrete-like ground with a large hammer; but the Lockewoods weighed down the corners of their tent and their guy ropes with stones, which they collected each evening. This reduced their tent size drastically and gave it a most *peculiar* shape. A more lopsided and sagging apparition would have been hard to imagine. I wondered how they managed once they had crept inside, and I dreaded what would happen in rain or strong wind.

With tactful encouragement from Adrian, our unwanted guests eventually pushed off; but the crackle of their footsteps through the dry vegetation died far too soon for comfort. Were they waiting just nearby? We retired to our tents wondering how far they had gone and how soon they might attack. I almost envied Turuwerk her freezing bed in the Ghia!

The next morning I was happy to realise that Callum's flea(s) must have stayed in Komboltcha for, during the night, no bloodthirsty insect had migrated across the tent from his sleeping bag to mine. It was a frosty night in a dirty site so everyone was glad to strike camp, but Thérèse was delayed by the needs and tantrums of Marthe who, in the way of infants, could no doubt sense our anxiety about the location. Her mother became irritable, and impatiently ordered our contingent to go ahead. Seven minutes later the Land Rover coughed and stopped. In the end we found a dirty carburettor had to be cleaned. The nasty Axum 'petrol' had fulfilled our fears!

We had gone perhaps another couple of kilometres when, rounding an outcrop we had to come to an abrupt halt. Right across the road was a massive Acacia branch: a classic ambush. Shocked eyes ransacked surrounding bushes. We couldn't *see* anyone – but that didn't mean they weren't there...

"Get rid of it," ordered Adrian in a tight voice as he braked but kept the engine running. "And be ready to hop onto the mudguard if I have to drive through it in a hurry."

In a daze of terror I obeyed automatically. The barrier was heavy and thorny but we never noticed our wounds. Expecting a volley of shots at every instant, Callum and I scrambled frantically to heave the monster off the road. We could only manage to drag it aside till there was just enough room for the Land Rover to get past, and even as we tried to kick a passage through remaining prickles Adrian charged the car over smaller branches and paused on the far side. When we moved off I was too agitated to speak but, in a croak which I didn't recognise, Callum voiced my terror by gasping: "Thérèse!"

"D'you think I'm going to give the bastards behind those boulders another chance while I demonstrate a three point turn?" shouted our white-faced driver. Despite all the tense moments this was the only time on the trip that Adrian used bad language or raised his voice.

In silence as thick as a pea soup we rumbled on. But when he found a suitably hidden spot Adrian turned the car and we faced the terror of squeezing past the barrier again. We'll never know why we weren't attacked. That Acacia branch had not fallen on the highway by accident. The tree from which it had been hacked was just a few metres from the road.

Concerned because the Ghia hadn't appeared, we found it stymied by the slight rise of loose stones back onto the road. Luckily, this being Africa, people – including repulsive lepers, poor things – materialised from the apparently empty countryside and pushed the car out of difficulty. They all scrabbled gratefully for a reward of small coins and sweets. Briefly we wondered if our callers of the evening before had been amongst the pushers.

Then what? To return and report the barrier to Axum Police would delay us at least 24 hours. The ambush had been un-manned twice today. Might it remain so for a little longer? – Very frightened, keeping the cars close together, we rushed round the corner and braved the fallen tree. Miraculously, again there was no attack. It was sometime later that I emerged from stupefied horror and started shivering from reaction. Scattered remains of the Acacia branch still lay on the gravel when we passed on our way home, nine days later.

Now we headed into a territory of vast ravines and gorges.

Although the Ghia seemed immune to Axum's dirty petrol, the Land Rover gave us grief several times during the morning. Every time we jerked to a choked halt my insides plummeted. Looking round the utterly desolate canyons I appreciated forcefully the dangers of being stuck in such a de-humanised region. Despite the chap who was taking sanctuary at Axum, and perhaps because of the failed Acacia ambush, I had now begun to consider that *Shifta* were a myth; but the horror of possibly being stuck so far from water or help, or any kind of human life, was terrifying. It's difficult to describe the intense 'nothingness' that simmered from steep, bare, rearing mountainsides and gaping chasms. Unless you have experienced miles and miles without vegetation, without a village, no hamlet, not even one small, teetering shack and never a single person, it's probably impossible to imagine the isolation.

However, most of the dirty particles in the Axum petrol must have been heavy enough to settle in the bottom of the tank for after lunch the Land Rover no longer had jolting spasms that ended in sudden halts on perilous slopes. We were sincerely grateful for that.

Hitherto, several times a day, we had alternately climbed to temperate cool climates, subject to frosts and mists, and plummeted down to steamy or scorching tropical climes. We had crossed one tremendous mountain range after another with vast dun-coloured plains between them. Now there were no more plains. The road became tremendously mountainous. Again and again we scraped a long way up, and then almost as far down, steep, arid escarpments so immense that their enormity seemed nightmarish. We were ascending steadily back into the heart of the Ethiopian Highlands. Vegetation changed from spidery Acacias and grotesque Euphorbia trees to scraggy bushes and a greener, more lush, type of Acacia. Yellow flowers, like extra-large cowslips, scattered the road edges.

A couple of little churches, several small war cemeteries and assorted monuments reminded us of the historic presence of Italian forces. Sadly all were in various stages of disrepair and some had been defaced. We traversed fantastic gorges, and had continual views of oddly shaped, square, and spiky mountains like the scribblings of a child. They rose in dramatic ridges very aptly described by David Buxton as: "A chaos of inextricable complexity!" These were the famous, rugged Simien Mountains, that hid Ras Dashan.

Simien Mountains

"A chaos of inextricable complexity."

That Sunday (8th) we lunched at the bottom of one of the incredible ravines, 5km wide at the top and about 2000m deep.

Pause for a second and take in those dimensions. That's the sort of extravagant terrain Ethiopia offers routinely. Gigantic gorges and vast plateaux go on and on... and on.

Here, on the banks of the wide, sultry Takkaze River we were at the lowest altitude of the trip: 1000m above sea level. It was appallingly hot and airless. Our seemingly unending descent to the Takkaze, which took several *hours* of coiling and winding track, was indescribably empty of buildings, humans and also, until we reached the river itself, of vegetation. It was a place of amazing, rude beauty, of desiccated, red earth and tremendous boulders. Fold after fold of threatening mountains led us lower and lower till we reached a bridge and started up the further, equally daunting, side. That bridge came as an abrupt surprise. In the middle of 21km of *absolutely nothing*, it seemed so incongruous that it was shocking; but without it we couldn't have crossed the swiftly flowing, and very wide river.

The Takkaze pours into the Atbara River that joins the Blue Nile south of Khartoum. I find it almost impossible to visualise the colossal dam, the highest in Africa, that was completed in February 2009 across this overwhelmingly immense valley. The influx of humanity that the construction, and all that this entails, introduced into the region, that was so *completely devoid of virtually everything* is also staggering to contemplate. The canyon 'slopes' are so deep and steep that major collapses, and thus sedimentation, almost immediately started to cause problems; and in 2008 the first massive landslide – due to eroding, vertical sides – forced developers to spend millions on retaining walls.

When in January 1961, like an insignificant beetle, we slipped and slithered down the tremendous canyon we were really at the *utter*

93

back of beyond. Few people had even *heard* of the place. Despite the appalling heat, the river water was cool. Keeping to shallows to avoid crocs we immersed ourselves gingerly. Marthe would have made a tender appetiser. Was it better to create a noise to frighten off the reptiles or to keep as quiet as possible so as not to advertise our presence to *Shifta*? Having experienced the desolation of this landscape I wondered that anyone, even bandits, could survive here.

{And yet, a year later when, with one female friend, I ventured again into these desolate parts, we discovered beside the river a small lean-to with a bench under a roof of banana leaves. An ancient, bent-over fellow sold tiny glasses of tea to rare travellers. We stopped, and, sitting on his rough seat, partook of his brew and wondered how he could possibly survive. The river had plenty of water so presumably he grew all that he needed; but it must have been a desolate, desperately lonely life. Was he an ex-*shifta* in hiding? – or even a still-practising guerrilla?}

After lunch I went for a tiny ramble and disturbed a couple of crocs. As such creatures do, they rose up onto their surprisingly long legs as if the reptiles' hides were being rapidly pumped full of air. Then they ran quickly down the sand and slipped silently, evilly, into ochre-coloured bubbles that swirled along on brown water. I saw what was probably a crocodile nest but I didn't have the time, energy, or courage to scramble through the underbrush to investigate. Pythons down here grow to great lengths, and croc mums sometimes stay on guard beside their broods.

Adrian's rough repair of the Ghia had lasted much longer than expected but now the car was lifted up (using stones and the Land Rover jack as well as that of the Ghia). The two men disappeared under the sports car clutching the parts scavenged in Axum. There were grunts and mutters. I passed implements and bits of wire. With Callum's brute strength and Adrian's know-how the car was patched up and we began the long, long climb scaling tortured loops on the other side of the Takkaze Gorge. We were impatient not only to leave the sweltering valley but also to reach the highlands and find a village from which we could hope to start walking.

8

BACK ON THE ROOF AGAIN

On we went – climbing and dropping, but mostly gaining altitude till ahead reared the shocking wall that sets Ethiopia apart from the rest of the continent. Grinding up those cliffs was a life-changing experience. Three days ago, at the Termabar Gap, we had plunged *down* off the Roof of Africa and since then we had continued less abruptly down, up and along the dramatic scarp's flanks. Now we were faced with the formidable effort of getting *back up* to the plateau. It's difficult to do justice to those mind-blowing cliffs.

The renowned Wolkefit Escarpment, with scores of squeezed bends, following in close succession, took the vehicles 2438m *almost vertically* upwards. *Blasés* though we had become of views and heights, we nonetheless gasped at the hairpins and at the unbelievable panoramas over great expanses of convoluted mountains.

These days, I suppose, a fine, smooth-surfaced highway, loops up in gradual curves. No doubt drivers still gawp at tremendous views and awe-inspiring drops; but rising in well-sprung comfort, today's travellers probably never give a thought to the sweating Italian soldiers who hacked a narrow, winding shelf from the desperately hard volcanic rock. To construct the last 16 km of the ascent the Italians had to literally hang from ropes over dizzy drops in order to painstakingly carve a road out of sheer cliff: an astounding piece of engineering! It took courage simply to drive up that thin gravel track, perched as it was on the uttermost *brink* of an immense void. Driving down, some days later, was simply *blood curdling*.

Near the top stood a large and tragic, monument which recorded the cost in lives of this steep, twisting road. The names of the men who had died building it were carved in several sad columns. A heart-wrenching inscription announced, in Italian: "We have not died in vain." I wonder if modern road builders have left that tragic memorial, or has it been destroyed? To us it was particularly moving to realise that people *had* been here in this wildness where we hadn't seen a human being in *many hours*. We, in our cranky, old Land Rover and nursing the boiling Ghia, had plenty of time to remember those heroes and to wonder at their bravery.

In this region, demarcation between desert and mountain was emphasised. It's this difference in altitude that kills camels attempting to reach the plateau-land of Prester John. They and their drovers suffer from lack of oxygen, and miss their customary food. They are not used to rock-infested routes and steep slabs which have to be negotiated. This is also the drop that sends highlanders' horses and mules plummeting into ravines, and suffocates, in desert sand and drought, the few survivors that manage to reach lower levels,.

These grandiose bastions that once protected Ethiopia from the surrounding scrub plains still exuded an aura of mystery. Part of this was due to the dark colour of the boulders. Some of the spell came from the gradually changing flora and from swirling mist near the top – so different from the parched environment from which we had risen. Water trickled out of black rock faces, and we passed fountains decorated with allegorical symbols of Italy and Ethiopia. At one curve with a vista that was exceptional, even for this unending precipice of incredible scenery, the Italians had constructed a more elaborate circular fountain. Ferns and flowering plants spilled over hard basalt. I relished the vision of over-worked road builders being

 allowed to express their artistic tendencies in erecting this attractive pausing place. Perhaps they sang opera as they worked. Now Gelada Baboons, perching on the surrounding perpendicular rocks, 'owned' the site, shook their huge manes and shrieked furiously at us.

A yawning Gelada Baboon reveals huge fangs and exposes a remarkable expanse of red gums.

At the top of the climb, after three hours of solid uphill labour, we passed almost invisible remains of an old Italian fort, where, in 1941, 3000 Italians had surrendered to the British. Now we needed sweaters; and we pulled long trousers over our shorts. By early afternoon having re-gained the Roof of Africa, we reached Adi Arcai, the capital of the Adi Arcai District. This was shown on the map as the most important hamlet between Adigrat and Gondar so Adrian had hopes of starting to walk from here. It was not a prepossessing place. A conglomeration of stone houses, in less than good repair, clustered untidily round the home of the village leader who had the grand title of "Governor of Adi Arcai". It was here that the Lockewoods intended leaving their infant in the well-meaning but moronic care of Turuwerk. Seeing the filth, the flies, the eye infections of the children, and the total lack of any suitable lodging my heart fell; but neither Adrian nor Thérèse turned a hair.

"Marthe can sleep in the car with Turuwerk and play with the Governor's children during the day," declared Thérèse brusquely when I voiced my fears. I glanced, shuddering, at the filthy, almost naked children and at their sores.

The pock-scarred District Chief, proud of his battered topee that marked his important position, turned out to be genial and readily promised to supply us with mules and a guide. But he insisted that he would not let us leave without a police escort. We didn't want to be bothered with a retinue but...

"The *Shifta* are dangerous," he said.

'Why,' I wondered silently, 'is this apparent myth of *Shifta* maintained?'

All the polite talk took time. When we decided to pitch tents and set out the next day we were invited to sleep in the remains of an old Italian building right behind the Governor's home. Before the village houses surrounded it, and before it started to crumble, this ruin must once have been a pretty habitation with the Italians' gift for selecting an excellent view. Now it was an overflowing public latrine that reeked to the point of making us feel sick; and the overpopulated area all round was disgusting.

A gibbet stood gauntly in the middle of this revolting scene. Contrived from three still fresh-looking Eucalyptus trunks, and like a large net-less football goal, it was of the type that was common in Addis where criminals were regularly strung up as a deterrent to other potential thieves and murderers. We were told that two *Shifta*, who had been caught as they attacked a caravan, had recently been hanged from the ragged ends of rope that still hung from the crossbeam. Even as my lack of faith in the very existence of bandits received a jolt, I wondered why the bits of cord had not been scavenged by the deprived folk of this village. Maybe they were superstitiously afraid of touching such remnants. Appalled by the scaffold and the filth, we said, as politely as possible that we wanted to be near a stream; and told that this was some distance from the village, we promised to return the next morning.

When we had set up camp in a pleasing spot beside the small flow of water, Adrian and Callum went back to be sociable and to offer the Chief some cognac as an inducement for him to speed up the procurement of mules and guide. We never found out what went wrong. Perhaps the local chief was offended by our refusal to camp in the sewer behind his house. He was extremely curt and said there were no mules, the route to the mountain was very bad, no-one knew the way, no-one had heard of Ethiopia's highest mountain... and so on. He ordered us to proceed to a village called Debarraque where, he claimed, we would find all that we needed. Thérèse and I opined that it had been lack of feminine tact that had upset the Governor and we swore to go into the village at first light to put things right.

The next day, before calling on him, we made a foray to see if the local souk-cum-drinking shop sold any kind of bread. The storekeeper, his clients, and the loungers all round, replied to our tentative enquiries by confirming the no-mule, bad-route, unknown-mountain rumour. This was current everywhere. Either it was true or the Governor had given instructions that the story should be spread. Accurate or not, our prospects looked bleak. Remember: there were no maps, let alone hiking maps. We couldn't set out totally ignorant of what we were aiming for or of where it might be.

As, in a depressed group, we discussed what to do, a man, apparently more civilised than the rest, and who spoke English, drove in from Debarraque. He had heard of Ras Dejene, which, he said, was the mountain we were seeking, and assured us that in his village we would find mules and an easier path to the highest point of Ethiopia. Perhaps he was just being polite, trying to be agreeable to strangers, but obviously he had not yet been contaminated by Adi Arcai's prevailing animosity; so we were inclined to believe him. We therefore left the Governor unvisited and unblessed, returned to camp, and set off for Debarraque with all possible speed as if shaking the dust of Adi Arcai off our wheels.

9

DEBARRAQUE

Debarraque, which we reached in time for a late lunch, turned out to be a large pleasant village – as such places went – with an unusually spacious market area surrounded on two sides by *toukuls*, and on one side by a row of small but well-stocked corrugated iron souks, owned in the main by Arab-speaking traders. The fourth side of this marketplace boasted a mosque. The man who had visited Adi Arcai lived in Debarraque and was, it seemed, a dresser, with some knowledge of First Aid. It appeared that the Governor of Adi Arcai had done us a favour by passing the buck (us) on to Debarraque.

We located the headmaster and gained admittance to the school compound which turned out to be enclosed and with a pump that produced *apparently* clean water. (Typhoid and other germs

Village children.

would be far too small to be seen.) Here Turuwerk and Marthe could stay comfortably while we were away.

It would be a Good Thing to organise mules and guide before visiting any bigwigs. But alas! The tribesmen seemed willing and pleasant, yet not a single mule was available. All we could procure were two tired horses, one with a blind eye and the other with a nasty sore on his withers. Looking at the abject poverty of the people, the bony goats and the surrounding overgrazed fields, I realised why there *were* no beasts of burden. Although at first he had obviously not even heard of Ras Dashan, or Ras Dejene as they seemed to call it here, a chap, willing to act as 'horseboy', promised he could guide us to that mountain. I was convinced that two horses, would be insufficient but because I had never trekked with pack animals before, I made only a couple of remarks and then remained silent.

The Lockewoods said they preferred to visit the headman alone so, as I didn't enjoy the bowing, scraping and endless discussion, I returned thankfully to the school where a small crowd of schoolboys had gathered round Callum. They were a pleasant bunch, who spoke English well and were pleased to answer questions about their schools in Debarraque and Gondar. They walked us across country to view an old church, and when we returned, the Lockewoods told us that they had secured permission to attempt the trip to Ras Dejene/Dashan but that two policemen had been detailed to come with us 'because of *Shifta* danger'. (Ras = Head.)

Of course there was no electricity but, until sunset, the boys organised a ping-pong competition and I marked exam papers! It surprised us what a difference the proximity of Gondar made to the people of this village as compared to the disagreeable folk in Adi Arcai, which was, roughly, only a mere 30 miles further from the town.

Although the drive from Addis to Debarraque had been wearing, we had seen some amazing vistas and enjoyed plenty of happy moments. Nothing terrible had happened en route so now it was pleasing to feel that the first part of our trip seemed to have been accomplished satisfactorily. *Turuwerk* was delighted that here she would be able to buy *injera* and *wat*. We sorted baggage and prepared loads.

In the school yard we cooked over a fire using wood we had collected during the day from a dead, roadside tree; then we pushed the desks in one of the large, airy classrooms to one end of the room, and all six of us slept well on the cement floor. Optimistically we planned to set out at 7am the next morning: hopefully to find, and, possible, eventually to climb, our objective. We never envisaged the difficulty of some of the terrain; the bitterness of the winds, the freezing nights, and how we would be feared and sometimes violently rebuffed by the few hamlets that we passed. Little did we realise how diabolically the horses (poor beasts) would react to conditions we were about to encounter. But all those horrors are for the next section – the actual walk. All I'll say here is that we had a supremely eventful expedition; we did manage to reach Ras Dashan, and to return, worse than filthy, utterly exhausted – but safe, and with an interesting story to tell.

A lady spins thread which her husband will weave into material to make their clothes.
{Pic of weaver on page 135}

PART TWO – THE WALK

These cliffs seemed to glow a vibrant deep viridian.

A very good bit of path

CROSS-SECTION OF THE WALK

The gradients were something as shown below. Of course, it wasn't all in one vertical plane.
We walked mainly South and South East at – very approximately – 2.6 km/hr and covered 115 km in all.

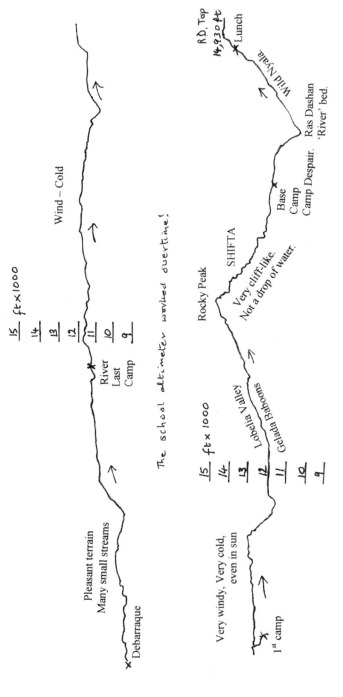

The school altimeter worked overtime!

FIVE & A HALF HARD DAYS

How naïve we'd been to expect the 'muleteer' to arrive at 7am! We scoured the place for him and sent small boys beetling off in many directions – all in vain... But he turned up at last. As foreseen, we had too much kit for two broken-down horses, so a third pack animal was finally found and we set off sometime after 10.00, minus our police bodyguards, but plus a large entourage of excited, cavorting, shouting, village ragamuffins. The two askaris (Askari = Policeman/soldier.) joined us after about 20 minutes and our ragtag escort of urchins gradually peeled off.

I have no record of how Marthe reacted to our departure. Presumably this indicates that she made no fuss.

We set off. I couldn't believe my eyes when I saw that Thérèse was carrying a handbag!

Our guards were as reluctant to accompany us as we were to be lumbered with them. At first they were surly, silent and so slovenly that we were certain they would run rather than fight any potential thieves. Sarcastically, we secretly named them Bandit Basher and Shifta Shifter. They wore ragged greatcoats, which indicated their respectable police position in society; and boasted army footwear, not on their feet but strung round their necks, doubtless because they found bare feet less painful than boots.

Of the three horses, which we called Komboltcha, Quiha, and Axum (Fred, Burt and Joe for short), QuihaBurt was the only sound creature. JoeAxum was blind in one eye and gave a lot of trouble on steep slopes. Probably because he had a horrid sore on his withers FredKomboltcha was an absolute devil, who tried to wipe off his pack against every convenient rock and bush. As a result of this charming habit he broke both my tent poles so my first task that evening was to splice them. Luckily I had taken large supplies of string, which also proved essential for closing the Lockewoods' bags since they packed their things in sacks that didn't shut.

Giant lobelia, and a man in a *shamma* and 'jodhpurs', with a different type of straw sunshade.

Several well-beaten paths left Debarraque in various directions. The horse minder took council from a large number of loquacious onlookers who all suggested different instructions. Discussion veered back and forth for ages; but when finally the consultation ended with dubious consensus, we set off across very pleasant, undulating country. It was wide open because the terrain had been desperately overgrazed and trees massacred for fuel. The horses splattered without trouble across some large streams. Mountains made an attractive backdrop.

This didn't last long. Soon we climbed a short, steep escarpment, streams vanished, and then for five and a half exhausting days it was unremitting hard mountain hiking with little vegetation except for strange, high-altitude plants such as Giant Lobelia, St John's Wort and Giant Groundsel like those seen on Mt Kilmanjaro, Mt Kenya and in the Ruwenzories. Little humming birds flashed very beautifully in and out of the many bell-like blooms up the stalks. Lack of water was a constant worry.

We clattered down into small valleys, and struggled steeply up the further cliffs. We plodded round shoulders of great ranges, usually with a ravine falling away to one side and precipitous slopes on the opposite face of the gorge. If we topped a huge mass of red or black earth it was only to be presented with the sight of more vast lumps, piled one behind the other, many fitting ponderously between the curves of apparently endless supplies of ever-higher mountains. The views were utterly spectacular, wonderful and awe-inspiring, especially when realisation dawned that we would have to footslog over those gigantic obstacles.

Most gorges were like this – with scant vegetation and steep sides eroded into deep gulleys.

It was in 1970 that I first heard Ravel's *Bolero*. I had long since forgotten about life in Ethiopia and I certainly never thought about the Ras Dashan trip; but the music immediately conjured a pressing vision of bare Ras Dashan gorges: one after another coming into sight with still more ridges and abysses in the background. Now I never hear *Bolero* without imagining long, scarcely-observable lines of weather-worn guerrillas plodding narrow paths over those great rifts. Small figures in single-file, coiling their ways over promontories, negotiating across the heads of valleys, slowed by distance so that they seem to be just inching along: grey figures following each other, scraping the sides of plunging gulfs, winding endlessly, repetitively, round, in and out of unending canyons.

At the time of our trip large parts of Ethiopia, including this Ras Dashan region, were known only to the sprinkling of locals who lived there; and even *their* knowledge was patchy. They were familiar with just their own small scraps of gritty, parched soil from which they scratched a painful existence. In the harsh Ras Dashan region there were few people, and no picturesque mud huts fringed with Banana trees such as we knew in other parts of the country. No foliage softened the scene round very isolated clumps of stone houses, which were thickly walled against the cold. The primitive settlements – much too small to be called hamlets – had strongly re-enforced rock walls topped with thorns against marauding *Shifta*. We very rarely passed such widely separated groups of hovels, and saw hardly any pedestrians, but the 'guide-horse-boy' took every chance

106

to ask the way. At the little communities we were not welcome and people vanished into their huts screaming abuse; but pedestrians were helpful, if not always knowledgeable. Sometimes they set up long shouts across the chasms. In the mountains Ethiopians have a way of drawing out their words, and ending sentences by going up the scale with "Oo-oo-oo-oo! Oo-ooooo!" These calls travel weirdly but for long distances. Then, if we were lucky, echoing replies came bouncing back from rock to boulder. In fact the choices of route were so few that, more by luck than by the muleteer's skill, we did eventually reach our goal. The policemen plodded stoically behind, their rifles across shoulders in the manner of sticks used by drovers of cattle. Although at first we hadn't wanted their company, in the end we were very glad to have their help.

Each evening the horse-boy and the policemen, who had just one threadbare blanket each as their only protection, naturally wanted to find a village; but the first day we had to walk till after sunset before we came to a cluster of cold, bleak, inhospitable huts surrounded by the usual stone walls that were topped by thorn branches. The inhabitants, who had already closed the entrance with prickles, first ignored us completely and then, yelling imprecations, were only persuaded with great difficulty to allow our companions in – to cringe behind

Our retinue at breakfast.

an empty grain bin as some form of shelter from the icy blast. We *ferengis* had to camp outside the walls. It occurred to me to wonder: If these people were so terrified of passers-by why was our escort cowering away inside the 'ramparts' instead of guarding us against the *Shifta* that the villagers seemed to fear so much. But what these pathetically poor folk could possibly possess that any thief might want to steal was more than I could comprehend.

The 'horseboy', Gelata, and policemen thought we were demented because we always hoped (always vainly) to sleep near a village where we might be able to buy fodder for the horses. As far as our retinue was concerned the pack animals could forage for whatever they could manage to snatch when we paused to re-fasten bundles or when we stopped for the night. During the hours of darkness the horses

Re-tying BurtQuiha's load on the first day.

were hobbled and we prayed that there were no hyenas about.

The route took us along not unreasonable altitudes of between 3050m and 3660m above sea level, which did not cause much loss of breath so long as we were not ascending. None of us will ever forget one nasty, boulder-strewn, 4489m peak which we had to surmount; while the height of Ras Dashan itself, originally recorded as 4633m, was in a 1970s survey reduced to 4550m. The cross-section of gradients is shown in the diagram on page 103. Of course, the walk was not all in one vertical plane. We travelled mostly south and southeast.

The mountains all sloped steeply and were very rocky so not until the very last night did we find a spot to camp that was even remotely level or 'comfortable'. The first site was particularly unpleasant. It lacked vegetation and the ground was rough, dusty and eroded. As a rule the Lockewoods used a lamp off the Land Rover battery so they had no torch; and as they hadn't brought candles they blundered around inside their floppy tent making it change shape like a monstrous octopus moving evilly in the dusk.

The 'guide' brought us some water, which was worse than filthy! He wouldn't show us the source so we couldn't fetch more after he had disappeared for the night. We boiled it well and disguised it with soup, cognac and fruit juice. In spite of the disgusting liquid, the inclined, uneven ground, the wind that made our canvas crack like clippers in a gale, plus the slight doubt about *Shifta*, we were all so tired that we slept very well. I was surprised and relieved that the Lockewoods' extraordinary shelter survived the blustery weather.

In these days of camping comfort when excellent equipment is easily available it's hard to credit the terrible gear that we took for granted. My tent was home-made. I had never heard of 'mountain boots'. Bed rolls were made of kapok, heavy, bulky and not nearly warm enough. I shudder to remember that when there was no fuel for a fire, our cooking was achieved on a temperamental primus – if we had paraffin!

The water situation was serious. While the Lockewoods had been talking to the headman in Debarraque, Callum and I had packed stores for the walk. We did this partly to be helpful, and partly because bitter experience had taught us that if we left the organisation of supplies to Thérèse we wouldn't have much to sustain us on the hike. However, to our horror, she unpacked it all. In the process of repacking she mistakenly left out the water bag and the second bottle of paraffin for the primus. This meant that on the return we had to find fuel for cooking – and there was desperately little to burn. Like our companions, bit by bit as we progressed during each day, we sought and salvaged dung and twigs and even stray leaves.

The lack of water bag was even more dire. It left us with only three bottles which was dreadfully inadequate since walking in the sun and wind made us all, especially the men, painfully thirsty. Such trickles as we found were rare, and had often been polluted by sheep and goats. Adrian became so desperate that sometimes he drank from these insalubrious sources – and he suffered in consequence. On the second morning we discovered the "spring" from which the previous evening's filthy liquid had been collected. It dribbled so slowly that the tiny muddy depression below the drip had completely dried up by the time we had horrified the villagers by an exhibition of the very minimum of cleanliness. There was nothing with which to wash our faces but supper saucepans had to have at least a token wipe. Then we waited impatiently while our three bottles filled frustratingly slowly drip by drop. And that was the supply for the entire hamlet!

This second day stretched on forever. It began with a contretemps between the Lockewoods who (falsely) accused the 'guide' of having pinched a blanket. The item found, we set off in high wind that sent dust flying. It stung fiercely. In December we expected no rain and were not disappointed, but even in the sun, and often, in spite of struggling uphill, it was bitterly cold. This was the day we had to overcome the particularly high ridge. Whether no path existed or whether the villagers had misled our 'guide' or merely not helped him with directions, we didn't know, but there came a time when we were battling up a pathless, boulder-strewn shoulder towards what we hoped would be the top of an escarpment. It wasn't only a 'killing' effort but it was also very frightening. Completely lost, we prayed that from up there, perhaps, we would be able to re-orientate ourselves. The going was really treacherous, and thirst was ravaging. The once-scary, possible attack from *Shifta* faded into insignificance.

To our left burst a magnificent display of mountainous lumps.

Thrusting suddenly skywards from a series of descending plateaux that were pink, blue, brown, buff, mauve, and green, they stretched eastwards towards cliffs and plains that we had toiled over on our way from Axum, Adowa, Takkaze… The extraordinary shapes of these immense protrusions had been dramatic last evening in the sunset, and now they seemed impossibly fantastic as the morning sun caught their flanks and revealed expanses of almost luminous, dark-bottle-green cliffs, black precipices and umber slopes. They were *amazing* – a feast of unbelievably-jumbled peaks.

As we climbed, rocks such as these turned into a bedlam of boulders.

But very soon superb views were ignored. We had eyes only for the horrendous boulders, the size of cars and buses, over which we were battling. They were tumbled like bricks of a child's smashed castle. Scrabbling, gasping, slithering, clawing round unyielding lumps... used so much energy that, despite the wind, we stripped off outer layers of clothing. Callum even removed his shirt – and was in agony later. Being extremely fair he burnt to a painful, blistered puce and peeled horribly.

Our pack animals couldn't cope. We had no option but, time and again, to unload the three wretched horses and, going back and forth, carry camping gear and food ourselves. Yet, even with nothing to carry, our intended beasts of burden could scarcely conquer the gradient or surmount cascades of great vertical chunks of toughened basalt. It was hard enough for humans, who could use hands. The policemen, who had been forced upon us, were now very useful.

In the lead one of our two scrawny, barefoot, anti-*Shifta* worthies, struggled up the arid cliff with, like the rest of us, an assortment of unlikely items in his arms and others draped about his body. In his tatters, he looked more like a melodramatic theatre buccaneer than any real-life militiaman. Puffing in the thin air, Bandit Basher and I reached a place where we could stand side-by-side and listened briefly to the dreadful sounds of our 5 companions and the horses as they made incredible efforts to battle up behind us.

"Here! Take this!" My improbable policeman dropped his bundles, shoved the sack I was clutching roughly to the ground, and thrust his rifle into my hands; "and keep your eyes well-skinned for *Shifta*!"

Perforce I took the gun, though I wouldn't have known how to use it; and, still puffing, stationed myself upon an out-thrusting boulder, eyes peeled across scores of simmering ochre ridges for any suspicious movement. A young, scruffy, sunburnt female in skimpy shorts, I did my best to look menacing. Shadows along our current unending gorge were sharply-defined, purple-black depths that could have shielded hundreds of desperadoes. Elsewhere scorching sunlight reflected blindingly off towering crags. What would I do if I spotted an advancing column of ruffians?

My Protector disappeared downwards to help Gelata and Shifta Shifter who were quite literally pushing, pulling and shouting our horses up the cliff. The poor creatures, ears back, eyes rolling, kicked and scrambled, slipped and sprawled, sending rocks bouncing down the chasm. Echoes rebounded round the long ravine. The noise was thunderous and explosive beyond description. Any brigands within miles must have known of our presence. Was our shoddy troupe sufficient inducement for them to attack?

Half way up my right knee started to hurt, and a little later Callum's left leg became painful. We presumed that our muscles had been strained but, wearing crepe bandages, we were able to continue as the pain subsided and thereafter only returned from time to time. Adrian hurt his foot and, by the last day, it had swelled so much that he had to cut away part of his shoe.

The present nightmare ended (temporarily) when, exhausted, we reached the top of that grisly, rocky ridge, where we took note of a spire-like heap of boulders, and hoped that we would be able to recognise the pile to find our way back. Gelata beamed with delight and pointed, but the rest of us were almost too tired to cheer when we observed a lump which, he told us, was Ras Dashan. It was not only far ahead and across yet another deep valley, but it was also disappointing: a long, massive, looming ridge that poked up at one end to a flat top. We made out whiteness. Might it be snow? – Or ice? Perhaps we'd find out tomorrow. As far as we could make out its upper reaches were steep cliffs. Below those the sides spread out towards lower slopes like flares of a full skirt. Possibly we'd have found Ras Dashan more inspiring if we had not already been stunned by scores of previous spectacular summits, ranges and gorges on this trip.

First view of Ras Dashan. The top is on the right.

We were too cold to linger on the top of our current ridge and tried to decide how to descend the steep mountainside that dropped away below us. Here and there we spotted what seemed to be vestiges of a route threading the boulders, but these 'perhaps feasible' sections must have been quirks of nature and not paths because they were very short and interspersed by dreadful tumbles of huge tough lumps; so clambering down entailed more periodic unloading of horses, carrying our goods in relays, then returning to coax the pathetic, suffering animals down, to be re-loaded till the next impossible section made it necessary to unload and carry again. The endless unloading and re-loading became more and more shattering, especially when the incline was – as usual – abrupt.

113

We camped just before sunset at what we optimistically decided to call Base Camp. Exhausted, the Lockewoods and the policemen had dropped behind so Callum and I, with the 'guide' and horses, tried to locate a stream by which to camp. The slopes were swarming with goats clattering down rocky gradients to a parched, yellow, dusty expanse where we could see a couple of hamlets on a slanting area intersected by many small valleys. With so many goats and two, albeit miniscule, villages we felt that there had to be water in one of the depressions. But they proved as arid as the higher regions so we were forced to settle beside the one trickle that ran at about 40 drops per hour (allow for exaggeration!). An appalling, unappetising spot, it seemed to supply all the families and their livestock. There was *never* a daylight moment when there wasn't a villager patiently holding a container below the drip. And they resented our presence with a virulence that was terrifying but understandable since we were using their dribble of water.

Ras Dashan, was still a long way off, across a deep and wide ravine. As you'll see from the cross-section of the walk (page 103) we still had a steep descent before we actually gained the lower slopes of Ras Dashan, but we were cheered by the thought that we were now more or less at its foot, and started hallucinating about reaching the top.

The freezing wind howled, so we pitched our tents in a dry stream bed hoping its lumpy sides would break the blast. I felt desperately sorry for our escort who hunkered down behind a couple of boulders a bit lower in gully. For warmth and to scare off hyenas, every waking minute of every day, they scavenged whatever they could find in the grubby surroundings to keep a fire burning all night. They never complained, but it must have been a bitter experience.

Although hundreds of rocks were firmly embedded in the steep mountainside round our campsite, loose stones in our powdery, yellow patch were very rare. Perhaps the natives had collected them all to construct huts and 'fortifications'. We had a long and tedious hunt for anything that would weigh down the Lockewoods' tent.

We agreed to leave very early the next morning so Callum and I rose with the sun, but the expedition leaders refused to wake. Finally roused, they had trouble and argued loudly about something,

114

which they never imparted to the rest of us. We were only just outside their tent so, had we listened we'd have discovered what it was all about, but that seemed rude so, huddling in our jackets, we ambled out of earshot. Their tent, always amorphous, was more than ever like an amoeba as it bulged and then subsided in various places corresponding to their unusually violent gyrations inside. All this delayed matters dreadfully but after the long, tense setback, horribly late, we started off as quickly as conditions permitted, taking BurtQuiha to carry the lunch and to be available in case anyone needed help. Shifta Shifter was more than happy to be left to guard the camp and the other 2 horses. He also had instructions to rinse and fill, from the reluctant spring, all tins whose contents we had eaten. We hoped that this water would be handy for supper.

We had discovered that the inhospitable villagers en route were eager to swap empty tins for tiny eggs. The going rate was five eggs per tin so the more we ate the richer we, and our retinue, became – in very small eggs. But we saved four tins for ourselves and started each day with every person carefully carrying a tinful of water to supplement the 3 meagre water bottles. We gave our Ethiopians a tin each but these they quickly bartered.

Mid morning. A daunting prospect. We had to get onto that ridge and walk along it to the summit.

Our extended scramble down the deep ravine took time and care. At the bottom was the dry Ras Dashan River. Then we climbed a wide, long – long, L-O-N-G, upwardly-sloping valley in which there were 3 small and widely dispersed settlements. The

Lockewoods dragged frightfully and caused further appreciable delays, which aggravated Callum so much, that he dashed impatiently ahead, only to have to sit waiting and shivering. Bandit Basher stayed with them and I plodded centrally beside the 'guide' and BurtQuiha, both of whom found the altitude extremely trying. By 2pm we were still far from the summit. The horse and 'guide' were about done in, and the rest of us were feeling the 4000m altitude. We barely stopped for a few bites and to consider plans of action. Gelata and BurtQuiha were both very glad to be left to wait and freeze.

"That's the way," said Adrian pointing up a gully that started nearby. "It goes straight to the top."

Awesome view from a rest spot.

It certainly *did* appear to head towards the summit; but equally certainly it was definitely 'straight' – as in 'vertically' – up! It was very steep, full of ice, and looked *awful*.

"Why not try to work round the side of the mountain. It's not so precipitous that way. Then we can continue up the ridge," the rest of us suggested; but Adrian was determined, and off he went, foolishly. It's never wise to walk mountains alone, and that particular channel was quite evidently extremely dangerous.

We had approached the mountain from the north, where its upper reaches were cliffs. This was definitely the 'wrong' route. The best plan would have been to have arrived from the east and found the spine, which rose reasonably gradually westwards towards the

116

peak. The best we could now attempt was to traverse left (east) climbing as we went, hoping to reach the spine and then to turn right, and walk along the more gradual ridge that slanted up to the summit. But time was against us.

Occasionally, for a while, we could see Adrian slipping, and struggling desperately, to surmount the chaos in his chosen gully.

The remaining four (counting Bandit Basher) proceeded to climb, pant, and traverse, attempting to reach the sloping spine. But it was a devil of a long way to that crest. It became obvious that we would never make the peak and then get down to lower and less freezing altitudes by nightfall. So, when we reached a section which seemed to have fewer rocks and not to be so utterly perpendicular, Callum and I advocated climbing more vertically up this scree of huge, icy stones, making as good an attempt as possible, but definitely not going on and on until we were forced to sleep on the mountain. What a prospect! Temp below zero; constant strong, buffeting winds; rocks with a thin cover of frozen dew; patches of old snow, frozen on the ground; no food; no blankets; no tent; no firewood… No thank you! Dressed in cotton, with tennis shoes on our feet, we were not equipped for freezing conditions. Thérèse wouldn't contemplate our idea. Adamantly she insisted she would continue round the mountainside, gradually gaining height and then walk along the scarp edge to the top. Undoubtedly this was the most creditable route but we just did *not* have the time to attempt it.
"If necessary," she said. "I'll sleep wherever I am at sunset."
The three who were staggering along with her were horrified but couldn't dissuade her, so off she tottered, gasping, followed by a depressed and equally breathless Bandit Basher.

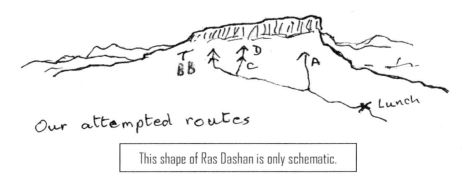

Our attempted routes

This shape of Ras Dashan is only schematic.

117

Callum and I turned off right and began to scramble up the cliff towards the summit. From our present position Thérèse's route was obviously the correct ascent but to tackle that we would have had to camp on this side of the Ras Dashan River's ravine, which we had crossed earlier, and take an extra day on each of the outward and return journeys.

Thérèse never attained either spine or summit. It was too far even for her; and she later attempted a nearly vertical ascent like ours. Being further round the ridge, her climb was shorter and less steep than our struggle, but eventually she had to turn back and battle downhill in the dark and without a torch. She and the faithful Bandit Basher ended up in a bleak village where the inhabitants first refused to acknowledge their presence, then swore at and spat on them, and finally left them to squat outside, in the lee of the settlement walls. They spent a perishing night with nothing to eat and scant shelter. The next morning they were given a horn of milk to share. They were so desperate for liquid that Thérèse swallowed her small portion with gratitude and gave no thought to its germs.

Somewhere near the top.

118

Callum and I climbed successfully, slowly – but faster than we had been able to move when hindered by Thérèse – up a series of huge, very steep, icy steps which alternated with rivers of rocks like "petrified waterfalls". Photos show that we were not far from the top when, alas, Callum developed vertigo. It was a bitter blow for we had achieved pleasing headway, and I could have continued for a good bit further. Probably he was also suffering from altitude sickness. Snail-like – with me supporting him – we proceeded little by little, but his state became alarming and it was now 3pm. It seemed stupid to push on. Even if we rushed like mad – always unwise – and even assuming that we would be able to descend faster than we had climbed, the trek back to camp would take several hours. So, regretfully, he rested against the cliff and I proceeded some way alone. My camera was jamming – probably because of the cold – but I tried to take photos, and then returned to Callum. We negotiated and edged our way down.

More by luck than by skill we found Gelata and BurtQuiha, huddling together and looking worse than miserable. We told the 'guide' to wait for the Lockewoods, took my torch and extra sweater

119

from the horse pack and then, hobbling as fast as our bandaged knees and the unpleasant terrain would permit, we tried to continue weaving between obstacles and slithering down the north face of Ras Dashan. There was absolutely no vegetation so views were unblocked. Before dark the three dispersed villages could be clearly seen so we used them as indications of where we should head, and intended to find the spot where we had crossed the bottom of the ravine from which we would then have to scramble back up to the camp.

Without Adrian, Thérèse and the horse we managed to double our previous speed and by superhuman effort we reached the Ras Dashan River by 6pm – sunset. Then began the steep and arduous climb which eventually brought us to the inhabited yellow 'plateau' – long after the sun had vanished. We were both absolutely exhausted and in quite a lot of pain. However, we now found a criss-cross of goat paths and imagining that we were not far from Base Camp, we hoped that we would bump into one of the hamlets. Maybe the unfriendly people would yield enough to tell us how to find The 'Polici Dunquam'. (Police Camp)

But before we had located a village we stumbled upon a valley that seemed familiar. What optimists! Thinking that we had miraculously discovered our valley, and that the tents would not be far away we trudged wearily towards a lump that appeared in the gloom. Could it possibly be the lone tree close to the boulders where the escort had slept? There were scarcely any trees around the region so the apparition was heartening. Surely it must be *our* tree? Were we close to camp? We slogged wearily towards the 'lump" but: – it was *not* a tree! That was awful!

Eventually we reached some *toukuls* where the folk were most unhelpful, and treated these two shouting figures, emerging from the dark, with great suspicion. They refused contact and, with insolent actions, added more spikes to the closed entrance of their thorn *boma*. On we plodded, seemingly on forever. Not sure of where we were heading... In fact it could not have been much more than half an hour later when we heard a horse clopping up in the distance, and hailed the rider to ask the way. To our amazement we were addressing our 'horse-boy'! He led us on to the tents that we had in fact been approaching. Our unsafe, scruffy camp was a joy to behold!

Callum claimed to be too tired to eat but I insisted on having something. We felt better with soup, mouldy bread and sardines inside us, and were able to prepare supper for the Lockewoods. After a while, however, it became apparent that they wouldn't be back in camp that night so we didn't wait up for them. I doubt that our eyes would have stayed open even if we *had* tried to stay awake.

Adrian appeared early the next morning, in time for the three of us to have breakfast together. He had no news of Thérèse or of Bandit Basher, which worried Callum and me, but her husband remained unmoved. He'd been completely lost and, at last, finding an inhospitable village, had slept under a haystack outside its walls. At dawn the villagers relented so far as to generously give him two raw eggs and a horn of *talla* (native beer) – riches indeed from these poor folk. The exterior of the horn was slimy with *talla* dregs of many previous draughts as the brewers obviously never washed their vessels. In view of the lack of water this was scarcely surprising.

Like Thérèse in her village, Adrian was too parched to be fussy, and he then amazed the entire local population, who stood round watching his every move, by begging an ember from one of their fires. With this he was able to light a handful of straw from the goat pen, make a blaze and then cook the eggs on an old bit of tin, which was lying among the chickens. He ate the eggs using a scrap of cardboard that he found underfoot. No doubt it had had its fair share of being kicked about by humans and goats. Adrian was worse than FILTHY! – even more disgusting than the rest of us, and that was saying something! As to the muck he must have consumed... It didn't bear thinking about.

When he came down from the mountain, having been beaten by that ghastly icy gully, he understood from Gelata that everyone else had gone back, so he set off for camp too. The 'guide' climbed onto BurtQuiha and went on ahead, soon leaving Adrian well behind. Meanwhile Thérèse and Bandit Basher, still on the upper slopes, saw the 'horseboy', a tiny matchstick figure, gird up his loins and his mount, and move off. Thérèse didn't observe Adrian at all.

By the end of a slow breakfast we still had no news of her. We were wondering what to do when Bandit Basher materialised at camp. Thérèse, he said, was far away. She was hungry and wanted 'headache medicine'. (The headache was probably as much due to altitude as to lack of food.) Very quickly we packed some bread, a tin of Spam (plus tin opener) and aspirins into a bag. The bread was mouldy but that was all we had. Perhaps the growth would act as Penicillin and fight germ-ridden conditions!

Many indigenous mules and horses refused to carry non-Ethiopians so we didn't know if our steeds would tolerate a European rider; but we tied a couple of blankets onto BurtQuiha to make a sort of saddle; Bandit Basher having explained where he should go, we sent the 'horse-boy' back to get her and Bandit Basher collapsed in a heap. The previous day BurtQuiha had been used with a negligible pack (apart from carrying Gelata home) so we reckoned that going to fetch Thérèse, and then perhaps carrying her, but for much of the time not carrying anything at all, would be less stressful for him today than later carrying gear back over the high, bouldery ridge.

We ought to have spent the day resting, but when had we been sensible on this trip? The thought of languishing for another day of howling gale, and suffering a second freezing night beside that dehydrated, loathsome waterhole filled all three of us with such disgust that we decided to strike camp. Callum and I, with Bandit Basher and the remaining two horses, would somehow manage to take our gear over the rocky peak and pitch camp in what we called The Lobelia Valley, which we had observed on the outward journey. That promised to be a delightful spot with vegetation and places where the ground was fairly level. The thought of leaving our present squalid surroundings and reaching The Lobelia Valley seemed like heaven!

Even though Bandit Basher had experienced an exhausting previous day we chose to take him instead of Shifta Shifter as he was the stronger and more agile of the two guards, and we knew that we would be carrying equipment and pushing/pulling horses over great boulders. When Thérèse and Shifter Shifta got back to Base Camp Adrian would explain our plans to Thérèse. The Lockewoods would be lumbered with hardly any luggage and have Gelata and Shifta Shifter to assist them over the high ridge. That was the plan, anyway.

The Lobelia Valley was not a great distance down the far side of the high ridge and we hoped that Thérèse would be able to sit on the horse whenever gradients made this possible. We intended to have the camp set up and supper ready for them. So Callum, Bandit Basher and I started off with one half-blind horse and another pack animal possessed of an evil spirit, all five of us grossly overloaded but glad to be leaving the abominable waterhole.

At first we had difficulty with the animals because they had become used to the 'groom' and were not inclined to recognise our voices. But after initial troubles the animals calmed down and we managed fairly well. Bandit Basher was an absolute treasure and achieved wonders. Several times we had to stop to tighten the packs. On steep gradients this was a difficult manoeuvre. Once we simply could not tighten the girth sufficiently so we had to unload JoeAxum and start loading him all over again. This, of course, was quite apart from the many times when we had to unload the horses because the gradient was so appalling. Each time we were then forced to carry up the gear bit by bit and finally haul the kicking, terrified, beasts up over the boulders, before re-loading. It was devastating work, but by now we had had practice and were becoming quite expert. At least the poor horses didn't try to escape while we abandoned them and carried loads. The ghastly boulders all round were enough to daunt any creature, and the pack beasts' incredible efforts had probably dazed them beyond any thoughts of escape.

From time to time today Bandit Basher just placed his rifle on a convenient boulder and did not indulge in melodramatic actions such as telling me to watch out for *Shifta*. There was no-one to spare to act as look out, and, anyway, *Shifta* were the least of our worries that morning. All this was not impossibly difficult on the lower slopes. Higher up it was horrible.

We were panting for oxygen and also Callum and I had to prospect to find a way that would be at least hang-on-by-the-skin-of-teeth-able for the pitiful horses. We had to try and pick the least-ghastly route round, between and over boulders. JoeAxum refused and baulked at every opportunity – and no-one could blame him. What those horses achieved would be difficult to credit, but somehow they did it – poor things! Once Bandit Basher actually had to stone JoeAxum to get him to move! It was very distressing but we had to get back somehow. How the horses' flailing legs were not smashed in the fearsome rocks was a miracle that I could never fathom.

123

Once Callum and I lost contact for an appreciable time. That was frightening. It was even worse for Callum because, periodically, he was overcome by vertigo and altitude sickness. If this happened to him when he was on his own the excruciating effects seemed magnified. After that we were careful to stay at least within calling distance as we sought for a feasible trail. It was a horribly desolate, freezing, rocky, cave-ridden mountainside. We swigged a sip of cognac for warmth and encouragement. Ahead our spire-like pile of boulders was like a beacon on the skyline but we never bothered to give Ras Dashan more than one tired, regretful backward glance.

Joe-Axum and Fred-Kombolcha thankfully survey a nice bit of path.

Eventually we scrambled, kicked and slipped our way up and round the edge of the peak. Then we had to repeat the dreadful pantomime on the descent, but this time we were able to choose a shorter route through the boulders because we were veering off towards The Lobelia Valley. Once at the head of that valley we sat down with songs and whistling to admire the splendid view and to let the horses graze. We were all malodorously filthy but what did that matter? We were alive, and we'd crossed the soul-destroying summit.

It was 2.15. We paused briefly for a quick, much-needed snack. My! That was a blissful moment!

124

It was a relatively easy descent three-quarters of the way down the valley. Here we found an excellent camping spot below a sheltering shoulder of hill. There was no village for Gelata and the Policemen but Giant Lobelias, bushy Giant Groundsel and other plants offered rudimentary shelter. It was also a place where the others would see our campfire when they topped the ridge. It was 4.30pm. We stopped, put up the tents and prepared supper.

What a camp that was! – right on the edge of a vast escarpment! Lovely grass underfoot, dried bits of plants for firewood, delicious water, a small flattish space for tents and a gorgeous panorama down an unbelievably enormous precipice to the plains where a million pinnacles, peaks and domes pointed up into the heavens. Oh Joy! We were amazed that no humans had despoiled the place with a village. That source of water was so superior to any other that we had seen. Why hadn't the 'guide' led us this way on the outward journey? He probably didn't know of the spot, and also we had been pressed for time and hadn't been in this vicinity at a suitable hour for ending a day's walk.

Not far away colonies of luxuriously-maned, raucous-voiced, grimacing Gelada baboons leapt about the rocks and made foraging parties down to the stream. They ate the trunks, and probably also the roots, of the Giant Lobelias. Some of the plants, at lower altitudes, were truly enormous and very tall, but at higher altitudes they shrank. When fleshy leaves of Giant Groundsel bushes grew on the edge of a rocky outcrop they then looked just like shaggy heads peeping at us over the escarpment.

The sun was starting to set as Bandit Basher, Callum and I scraped up the final crumbs of a slap-up supper of tinned Spam, mouldy bread and gallons of tea. We sighted the others. Thérèse, supported by Gelata, was staggering as she walked. Her legs were like jelly. She was absolutely whacked and went straight to 'bed'. She had refused to ride the horse. Conditions had made that too terrifying to even contemplate. Adrian cajoled her into eating some food and managed a few bites himself but he was so worn out that he also fell into 'bed' as soon as possible. They had had a slight tiff during the climb when, for some unexplained reason, the 'guide' and Thérèse had waited for Adrian in one spot while he and Shifta Shifter had been waiting elsewhere.

Giant Groundsel. When in bloom they had long spikes covered with purply-green florets.

It was uncanny how Giant Groundsel bushes seemed to be peeking over cliff edges at us.

Bandit Basher managed a second supper as the three Ethiopians celebrated by tucking into a mixture which – to me – looked foul, but which was doubtless delicious, and which must have been very nutritious. It was *tef*, mixed with a stick, in boiling water and eaten with fingers from a communal pot. I watched the preparation and eating, with great interest. Then, round the fire, the five of us stayed up late, drinking cacao and watching the stars that

126

always sparkle especially brilliantly when observed from high altitudes – and without competition from city lights. We talked, roasting on one side and freezing on the other.

Callum asked to look at one of their rifles.
"Is it empty?" he asked. To be certain of this he fired into a nearby bush. There was no result but a dull click.
"Where d'you keep your ammunition?"
The *askaris* shrugged. "No money. No ammo."
The policemen who had been imposed upon us as being so essential against possible Shifta had all the while been completely unarmed! What a waste of energy it had been carrying those heavy, useless weapons!

That night they named me 'Ambasa' (Lion), and were very complimentary about my walking skills. Callum had been given that sobriquet on the first day, chiefly because of his great size and his lion-like colouring. His ultra-blonde hair had golden lights and russet shadows. His eyelashes were so fair that they sometimes seemed to vanish. However, any onlooker would have been hard pressed to understand why we had been so honoured with the 'Ambasa' titles. We presented a ludicrous sight: Callum first, limping with his left knee, me next, limping with my right knee, Adrian hobbling behind with his shoe cut away to ease his greatly swollen foot, Thérèse unable to proceed without support and the rear brought up by a semi-blind horse!

The next day we plodded on and eventually made camp beside a rather smelly river – but at least the water was flowing! By then we had reached slightly inhabited regions and we felt that our walk was nearly over. But not so our troubles. The next morning Adrian was groaning, in great pain with diarrhoea, and could scarcely move. We dosed him with sulphur guanidine from my First Aid kit and hoped for the best, wondering whether Callum and I should try to go ahead and attempt, despite the terrain, to bring the Land Rover as far as possible to pick him up. Luckily Adrian was *most violently* sick and soon after that he was so much better that he could totter on.

The following day we got back to Debarraque in time for lunch at 13.30. We were spotted when still far off and streams of

127

children came running, hopping, skipping, waving and shouting to meet us. The adults in the village were astounded to see our party back so soon. To do the trip happily and in comfort I would advise anyone to take at least 8 days and perhaps to use riding mules as well. Horses, poor brutes, were definitely not suitable. We did the round trip in 5.5 days entirely on foot, suffering desperately from lack of water, and with insufficient and extraordinary pack animals which deserved much praise for their heroic achievements.

That Sunday afternoon was marvellous! We bathed in a stream. I washed my hair and all my clothes except the ones that I was wearing. Spread over the overgrazed land they soon dried. Marthe and Turuwerk were well and happy, but not ecstatic to see us.

The local schoolboys led Callum and me to a hut where a venerable man reported that, many, many years before, he had taken one *'ferengi'* to Ras Dashan. The *ferengi* had had a party of 15 porters and guards plus lots of mules. We wondered who that explorer might have been but the aged fellow couldn't remember a name or nationality. What a pity we had not met this old gentleman before we had started walking. He would probably have given our 'guide' useful information, and given us much-needed advice.

By the light of our hurricane lamp that evening I was back to marking exam papers, but I spared time to write a lengthy report which I hoped the village headman would keep safely and lend to later walkers who proposed to reach Ras Dashan. Had we received such notes our trip would have been infinitely easier and much more enjoyable.

POINTS TO PONDER:

In 1841 two French officers: Ferret and Galiner, journeyed to Ras Dashan. We have no details of their route or adventures.

It occurred to us that the high rocky peak, which had given humans and horses so much trouble, might have been a geographical boundary that separated two parts of the countryside, and the population. Until we neared that ridge there had been either a well-marked trail, or some semblance of route. The people were wild but not untamed. Once we had descended on the far side of that nasty ridge down to the dusty yellow 'plateau' where there were a couple of hamlets, the inhabitants were even more primitive. But here we again found tracks. On the high rocky ridge itself, however, and also as we approached it from either side, the paths vanished. It was the highest and toughest part of our walk and we developed a theory that perhaps the locals on each side just never bothered to cross it to make contact with the folk on the further side.

People will probably think that my report is grossly exaggerated. It isn't. It's taken almost verbatim from the diary that I wrote during, and just after, the adventure. It's almost impossible for people who live in the Developed World in 2018 to imagine the unequalled, barren aridity of North Tigray in the nineteen sixties. The poverty of the people and the god-awful conditions in which they lived were apocalyptic.

Nowadays tourists fly to Gondar and take organised trips to Ras Dashan. They fly back to Addis via Bahadar, Axum, Lalibela... Sanitised, accessible and with comfortable hotels, these now-famous sites have all become unrecognisable to folk who lived in Ethiopia in the middle of the last century. Today life is much easier but it has lost much of the romance that it had when simply to exist was a battle.
A debatable point maybe: It's a shame that 'Progress' has deprived later generations of the thrill of battling, discovering, improvising...

Snow which falls plentifully and often on the cold Simien Mountain tops stays there for months during the 'warm,' wet, 'summer' (end July to 27th September) but, surprisingly, in winter, although the *nights* are perishingly cold, it's the 'dry' season, so without protecting clouds, the mid-day sun melts the snow covering.

Yes – I know – you laughed when I stated that the Rains end on September 27th. Well, until the mid twentieth century they *did*! For months through July and August, sunlight took on a greenish tinge as tropical downpours slashed trees and turned streams into red, frothing, impassable torrents. The land bloomed. *Every*where bright yellow Maskal Daisies (a variety of Cosmos) grew in great profusion. In *dambos* (damp glades) pink-edged, white lilies with overpowering perfume sprouted fantastically. Elegant Flame Lilies curled into big decorative bushes, and plains were dotted with a special type of incredibly blue delphiniums which had the most unbelievably-wonderful scent I've ever smelled. They were the subject of a learned treatise written by an amazed Kew Gardens specialist. During September the rains tailed off until, on the 27^{th,} they *ended* –Yes! Just like that!

On that day every year great crowds of villagers clattered into Addis on little mountain ponies. Every rider and hundreds of foot sloggers carried long, slender blue-gum branches stripped of foliage but each topped with a tuft of bright yellow Maskal Daisies. These were laid tepee-like in a public square, and later burnt. The aromatic cone of eucalyptus poles was surrounded by a red carpet. Emperor Haile Selassie, accompanied by bigwigs and his fluffy little dogs, trod ceremonially round the carpet three times. They were followed by many chanting and sedately dancing priests in spectacular, sequined garments. Over their heads acolytes carried marvellous, brilliantly-hued sunshades of shining velvet.

That night hundreds of sparkles twinkled from surrounding mountainsides. Each was the fire of a *toukul* whose dwellers were celebrating Mascal – the feast of the cross – and the end of the Rains.

Takkaze croc running into the river.

130

PART THREE　　　　　**THE RETURN**

Before starting back to Addis, Thérèse, who was utterly exhausted, stayed with Marthe and Turuwerk in Debarraque, lying on her bed; while Adrian, Callum and I spent a fascinating day visiting ancient palaces and temples round Gondar. They are now very well known but we were fortunate to enjoy these haunts of 18th century rulers before tourists discovered them. We thrilled at thoughts of extraordinary lives led by the less than eight Europeans who penetrated the mysterious Ethiopian stronghold between the fifteenth and eighteenth centuries. The few adventurers who returned brought such titillating stories of barbaric customs that they were mocked and (falsely) accused of lying. (Read Alan Moorhead's *The Blue Nile*.)

Apart from the usual alarms, and 'excitements' with the cars, the return trip from Debarraque to Addis went as smoothly as could be expected and included a couple of interesting events. We marvelled at the brilliant Aloes, Red-hot Pokers and giant Euphorbias that had exploded into fantastic bloom since we had passed on the outward journey. I wrote my diary and marked exam papers every evening, and we enjoyed *injera* and *wat* in cheap local eating houses. There wasn't enough cash to buy anything less exotic.

After camping the first night in the tiny hamlet of Adi Buna we drove to Yeha, a village with fine examples of Tigrean buildings made of flat, well-fitting, yellow stones. It also boasted a large windowless structure like a huge cube with 12m-high (Yes - *12 metres!*) crumbling towers. Probably dating from 700BC, it had double walls, and was an ancient pagan temple with an "altar" and a crypt. Sacrifices to the great moon god, Almough, were offered via a pool in the centre of the building. The interior had once been entirely covered with inscriptions, a fragment of which we were able to admire in a small house where some very friendly priests took us to see their colourful robes and historic parchment books illuminated in the Ethiopian style. (Good people are shown full face and baddies appear in profile.) The clerics functioned in a reasonably modern church, which had been built within the temple compound. This new church was carefully painted and decorated, and lovingly cared for. Its main attraction was its strange architecture since it had an unusual quadrangular shape and two square squat towers reminiscent of the more ancient structure nearby but of a sort not seen elsewhere.

.From there, following directions scribbled on a scrap of paper by an Ethiopian friend, we tried to reach the Debra Damon Monastery on top of an *amba* that had once been a princely prison. As this entailed driving across trackless, rough country Thérèse left us to it and drove on towards Quiha. The Land Rover struggled to a place from which, in the distance, we could see the immense lump rising majestically with vertical cliffs all round. Bumping on over atrocious terrain we located a hamlet from which the manuscript advised us to get a guide. The place was absolutely deserted. Not even a curious goat peered round a stone corner. No chickens disturbed the dust. The emptiness was eerie. We were on the edge of a deep gorge and

Climbing into an *amba*-top monastery.

could see no path to the *amba*, which was still far off beyond the chasm.

We dithered, wondering how to proceed, till an unwary youth suddenly appeared round a house, carrying over his shoulder a primitive wooden plough of the type then used by peasants throughout Ethiopia. Startled into the stillness of a frightened fawn, he stood gawping. Two inquisitive women in his wake grabbed him as he attempted to escape. When we explained that we'd like the boy to lead us to the monastery he again tried to bolt, but the ladies persuaded (bullied) him to trust himself to our awful monster. To make room in the car, Callum and I moved out to sit on the Land Rover wings, and leaving his precious plough in the care of the women, paralysed with fear, the lad allowed the ladies to shove him into the vehicle. After a few minutes he recovered sufficiently to indicate how we could avoid the chasm by bashing across torrents and ploughed fields. Much further on, we reached another village. Here, liberated from the vehicle, the boy scooted off and vanished.

Luckily this settlement was not only inhabited but also the folk were friendly. It was suggested that we parked there and proceeded on foot to the *amba* – which, we were told, was a walk of about 2 hours. The whole village would have happily guided us, coming with us *en masse*. We could have camped and achieved the hike the next day, but we decided to return because we thought that Thérèse would become worried if we didn't appear to spend the night in Quiha.

I was sad not to be able to continue even though I, as a woman, would probably not have been hauled up the sheer, 100ft cliff to reach the monastery. Callum, wasn't very keen on the idea – perhaps because of possible vertigo, and Adrian suddenly lost all interest and declared (correctly, I have to admit) that the project was too ambitious for the time available. So somehow, rattling and slithering, more by luck than skill, we found our way back to the road and finally, late at night, reached Quiha, where Thérèse was already asleep and not in the least worried about us!

After a late start the next morning we had a scrappy picnic at the second scenic lake where men fish from reed bundles, enjoyed an amble, and discovered the remains of what must have once been a delightful holiday cottage of some Italian family. The bush had taken

133

over and a dikdik (small buck) bounded away as we approached.

Arriving at Komboltcha in the evening, Turuwerk and Marthe slept in the Land Rover and our funds stretched to the four of us squashing into just one of the cubicles of the *un*delightful Paradiso. No-one got bitten by any creepy crawly.

On the final day of the trip we lunched beside some hot springs in which we could easily have poached an egg. We didn't try that as the waters exuded extremely strong sulphur fumes. Picked out in dazzlingly-white ridges, the mineral-full crust was very beautiful in gloriously bright yellow, ochre and swirling dark green algae.

I reached home to be welcomed by an ecstatic but emaciated dog who had apparently pined and refused to eat. After the delighted greeting she suddenly turned her back towards me and maintained this performance of outrage for at least half an hour before relenting.

As for the monkey: Whiskers was evidently glad to see me but no loss of appetite was reported as far as he was concerned. He gambolled happily, leapt onto my shoulders and revelled extensively in a conscientious search for anything interesting in my hair. The horses followed me around and when, the next day, I sat in the paddock, still marking papers, Grölle, the powerful grey stallion, came and stood behind me breathing down my neck. He stayed there for various quarter hours on end and, knowing how fiendish he usually was, I expected to have chunks nipped out of my ears or neck; but he was perfectly angelic. Strange! It was obvious that the old devil and the other horses were pleased to have me back.

The last of the much-travelled exam papers were finally corrected and Callum kindly came round to help me achieve the tedious and tricky totting up of marks so that, by the skin of my teeth, I was able to deliver the results on Monday morning.

Then it was back to work for all concerned.

The top photo on the next page shows earthenware pots for sale by the roadside in Addis. It's hard to believe that such gigantic pots exist. They must be heavy enough when empty; and it doesn't bear thinking about what they weigh when full. The women of Ras Dashan region would have given their eye teeth to have had enough water to fill containers even 1/30th the size of these.

The legs of this village weaver are in a hole. His toes, through loops in cords, operate the warp (up and down) while he throws the shuttle across and back to make the weft.

SMALL EXCITEMENTS

L to R. From back to front:
Father (W. A. Heyring) Head of General Wingate School and British Council Rep. The Wingate School Caterer. Christopher and Wyndham, my brothers. H.I.M. Haile Selassie Emperor of Ethiopia. Dad and the boys feature in the following anecdotes.

My brothers had been playing on the school compound when the Emperor arrived, without notice – which he did from time to time – to inspect various aspects of the school. Today it was to 'vet' the catering for the boarders' meals. He saw my brothers on their bikes and called them over.

Note the *modest* form of currently-fashionable, skirt-like 'Empire Builders' shorts' which the boys are wearing. On his leg Chris had a spider bite which produced a sore covered in linear crusts. They made splendid geometrical shapes (!) that disappeared over a couple of weeks.

137

The first mini excitements.

When Father was transferred to Ethiopia everyone asked: "Where's *that*?" Having got there, we thought it incredibly wild and savage. The capital had only 2 shops! – One was a Greek grocer's, the other sold *only* trilby hats. Addis was perched up at a great altitude which, on arrival, made even young folk gasp if they exerted themselves. Of course our bodies adapted and that was only a transitory effect. Some of the tribes seemed very dark, burly and frightening to us who had hitherto lived only in Egypt and Europe. Being unable to speak the local language was also strange.

Our first mini-excitement hit us two days after we'd arrived. Our parents had been invited to dinner. My brothers and I were ready for bed when the *most appalling* din approached. In utter darkness, across the field and into our garden thudded a veritable horde of desperadoes all flourishing torches made from flaming branches. They advanced yelling something like: "Hoya HO! Hoya HO! Hoya, Hoya Hoya HO!" Ground shook beneath their concerted stamps. Half-lit, ghoulish faces gleamed. They were gruesome! *Terrifying*! Were blood-thirsty warriors about to set light to our tiny, all-*wood* bungalow? Our night watchman? Vanished! The back door banged! Attack from the rear as well? Our cook appeared. "Present," he said with outstretched hand; then he re-joined the yellers. – OH! The penny dropped. They were carollers celebrating a feast. We'd no money but, greatly daring, I opened the front door and offered our 'visitors' a cake which we'd found in the kitchen. Rejoicing became more energetic and overwhelming. Then the shrieking group proceeded to claim more 'presents' elsewhere.

Three midnights later the family was woken by horrendous, gurgling screeches and blood-curdling howls. Just 2 metres from my bedroom window, our garden fence was being hit by large bodies. The feeble wall of grass which separated our bungalow from wild bush swayed frantically, and the ghastly 'snickering' continued. To see what was going on we held lights out as far as we could. Hyenas were enjoying a disgusting, vicious battle. Revolting, sloping backs and coarse, spotted coats merged into a bloody mêlée of fighting beasts which tore at each other with jaws powerful enough to crunch through the most robust of bones and hides. They even devoured hoofs and horns. The next day bush and garden were flat, and gory.

Kokorro! Kokorro!

Down the African Rift Valley stretch many remarkable lakes. Famous as much for their fascinating geology as for fantastic fauna and flora, they have distinct characters, and very varied sizes and hinterlands. Ethiopia has a string of these wonderful spreads of water whose colours vary from murky brown to sparkling blue.

In the 1950s heading south from Addis there was a gravel/dirt road from which one could find tracks that gave intrepid motorists access to one or other of the lakes in that region. The road also passed a couple of Missions established out in the wild, and a handful of villages. Frequented by spear-toting tribesmen these hamlets were tiny, without any facilities and the epitome of scruffiness, with goats and cows wandering the single street between decrepit mud-and-thatch houses. One little place we called 'Mucky Corner' because it was always very muddy, and slippery to negotiate. Many years later, when signs were erected, we were amused to see that 'Mucky Corner' was called 'Macky'. These days its name is 'Meki'.

I was nearly fifteen when the family had a minor adventure at Lake Awasa, the fifth lake going south and therefore one of the more remote places to get to. Not far from this lake was the settlement of Sheshemane. Today it's a thriving town with all amenities that one could possibly desire. It even has an airport; but we knew it as just another collection of huts. It did boast a primitive 'sort-of' shop, and a man who said he could mend punctures and breathe (temporary) life back into derelict cars. The state of the roads and the antiquity of most vehicles ensured that he always had plenty of work.

After six uncomfortable hours on the 251 km of 'main' road, we bumped through Sheshemane village and located a winding track that we'd been told to use. Bouncing over its rocks and ruts for some time took us down to a huge, choppy expanse of muddy brown, which was enormous Lake Awasa. The littoral further along the lakeshore became wide and covered with overgrazed grassland, dotted with scrubby Acacias. We didn't expect to see anyone and we were not disappointed. Finding a suitable site, we soon had the tents up and a cooking fire organised, native fashion, round three stones.

One tent and the cooking fire. (I still have that big pot and the huge kettle! Useful for parties.)

Not far off were ten poles sticking up vertically from the ground and joined in pairs like football goals without nets. They seemed a bit out of place but we didn't worry about them. Had the locals been enjoying football matches on weirdly shaped pitches?

We always took a servant with us. He helped by acting as a guard or by lending brute force if we had a puncture (or worse – a breakdown), and he did the washing up (on the lake shore using sand as Vim); but his main duty was to watch the camp if we went swimming or for a walk. The first time that Gimbi came camping he shimmied agilely up a tree to try and bring down some branches for firewood. Having always lived in Addis where fuel was a rare commodity, he had no conception that dry boughs might be lying about, easily available, on the ground. He was all set to tear down strips of bark from the trunks of Eucalyptus giants – except that at the Lakes there were few of those imported trees. We showed him how to pick up dry sticks and his amazement was ludicrous! Terrified of what he thought were local savages the poor fellow spent the whole trip in abject fear, his face a nasty shade of grey; and he took the first opportunity to buy a spear, which never left his side. On subsequent trips we took Zeleka, our then garden 'boy' who was much more phlegmatic, and who spent many hours just gazing vacantly over the waters.

Sunrise at one of the lakes.

Danger of crocs kept us from swimming out to investigate a strange object that was floating at some distance from 'our' beach; but in a couple of days it was washed ashore and we saw that it was a fine, 6m-long, very-dead python. We dragged it up the pebbles and dreamt of python-skin bags, wallets, belts, shoes... Unfortunately, as days passed, our future leatherware started to PONG! We dragged the carcase further from camp and trusted that hyenas would dispose of it, but apparently hyenas are not partial to python flesh. They preferred the rubbish that we left in a pile outside the tents every night. Garbage was always gone by morning. No need to dig a pit!

We had hoped to replenish stocks by buying fish or even a scrawny hen from local people; but no-one came near us even though herds and their goat-boys were visible in the far distance. Later we learnt that we had pitched camp exactly on the terrain where neighbouring tribes regularly participated in deadly battles. Our tents were on blood-soaked land where locals only ventured to do combat!

When he was told of our adventure, Col. Wilson, who was in charge of this district, remarked: "Of course, hyenas and vultures usually clean up any mess. But you might nonetheless have tripped over a human bone or two. And, also, that spot where you had your tents – That's where we hang chaps who've been condemned to death. No-one would dream of approaching that site unless they had war on their minds."

"Five of 'em were strung up just a week before your camping trip," he went on cheerily: "Perhaps you saw the remains of the gibbet poles?" We shuddered as we remembered the five net-less 'football goals' near our camp.

After several days in utter wilderness, we began to think of Sheshemane as a 'great metropolis'! So, as we'd had no fishing success, it was decided that a shopping expedition would be in order. My father, Gimbi and my brother Wyndham (aged seven and a half) set off in the car leaving Mother, my brother Christopher (nearly six) and me in charge of camp. All went peacefully until we spotted a posse of men, armed to the teeth, approaching along the sward.

Their spears glinted, and machetes were in evidence. They even had a few antiquated rifles that would probably hurt the firer more than the intended victim.

When it became obvious that the troupe was heading towards us my mother said in a tight voice:

"Hide the cameras."

We shoved our possessions into the tents and pretended to read in an unconcerned manner. The little squad kept on coming.

"Stop staring at them," Mother told Christopher. "Come here. Stay near me."

The platoon kept on advancing – at a fast pace indicative of serious intention. In forceful, guttural tones the men kept on croaking: "Kokorro! HUH! Kokorro! Korkorro! HUH! Korkorro! Kokorro! HUH! HUH!" The rude chorus implied that they wanted something, and they wanted it badly!

With the noble intention of protecting his women, Christopher – currently the only 'man' amongst us – vanished into a tent and emerged clutching his little airgun. Sometimes the boys had luck and supplemented stocks with an unwary dove or wood pigeon. Chris was promptly told: "Put that away. It will only make matters worse!"

142

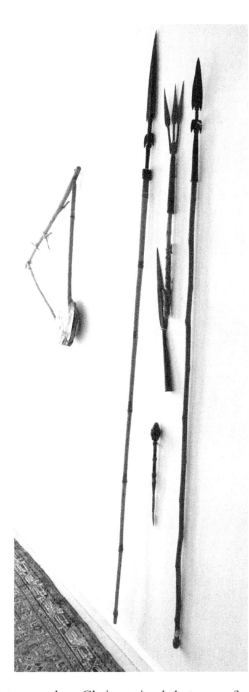

Indeed! The warriors were now all round our camp and drawing closer. We had absolutely no chance against those tough chaps with their forest of spears.

"Kokorro! HUH! Kokorro! Korkorro! HUH! HUH!"

The chant was pressing and depressing.

They swaggered nearer. "Kokorro! HUH! Kokorro! *Korkorro*! *Kokorro*!"

It was extremely intimidating. We could smell the rancid fat on their bodies and the chilly powder that they used in their spicy food. One of them had a long cockerel feather in his hair. Their eyes glittered.

They got closer. What on earth could we *do*?

Apart from the small Nubian stabbing weapon (centre bottom) these murderous spears and spearheads were acquired in various parts of Ethiopia in exchange for clothes, empty tins, packets of salt and such like. Waldi, who features in the *Coup* report, used to play the Krar (like a lyre) which is seen beyond the spears. Its bowl is an old metal basin – made in China – covered with cowhide.

"Kokorro! HUH! Kokorro! HUH! HUH!"

Things were definitely very tense when Chris noticed that one of our 'tormentors' was poking his spear towards the pile of empty tins, which we had been planning to

143

give to any scavengers who came our way. Containers of any sort were precious commodities. My young brother picked up a couple of cans and offered them to the now-tight circle of men. Their eyes gleamed even more, and several of them competed roughly to snatch the valuable objects. We now understood that 'Kokorro' meant 'tin'. They wanted ours.

Trying not to sound relieved, Mum told Chris to offer the rest of the empties to our fearsome visitors. Waving spears, and with astounding prances of joy, they seized the cans and uttered shouts of delight. Just as the pile had been (rapidly) demolished, our car came bouncing into view. Glancing uneasily at this approaching monster, our 'friends' reformed into good order, and continued marching towards whatever objective they'd been heading for prior to calling upon us. Col. Wilson told us that another violent and gory tribal battle had been joined that day; but, strangely, it had not taken place at the usual site. For that we were, indeed, thankful!

Mother couldn't bear to abandon her chance of python-leather luxuries so the snake's corpse was tied to a pole which was attached to the roof rack. Our olfactory organs suffered as the disintegrating body jet-propelled us back to Addis. Sadly, although the tanners did a good job, the skin was too damaged and holed by spear thrusts to be used. Now, 67 years later, it's very fragile but it still hangs on the wall of my garage and invariably amazes plumbers and others who come to undertake repairs.

The python skin is actually horizontal on the wall.

Lake Shala

Father lost 2 valves and Christopher lost his pyjama trousers. These 'momentous' events happened when the tents were beside our favourite lake: Shala. It was the only lake whose waters were really blue and it sparkled like a bag of well-cut diamonds: a brilliance which was partly due to the minerals in its very alkaline waters.

"Ah! Lovely!" declared Father as he was emerging from a dip after we'd pitched camp. He rubbed moisture from his hair and we all stared! His head was engulfed in thick foam as if he was enjoying a very soapy shampoo! He looked like a surreal Father Christmas. The mixture of natural hair oils and lake chemicals produced this astounding effect every time anyone had a first swim at Lake Shala.

The family camps at Lake Shala. Wyndham watches Dad carving a piece of wood. Chris digs a long native spear into the ground. Mother's big sunhat shows her emerging from behind the small sunshade-tent. Zeleka is washing up on the beach. I am painting the picture but I have put myself (indistinct) lying under the canvas canopy – reading. The Austin is behind the canopy.

No fish could survive in Shala's strange water so there were no crocs either, but there were both in the small river that flowed into the lake and provided a water supply, which we boiled well before drinking. One of our favourite camping spots was beside that river even though we had to cross the flow to reach a smooth area for the tents. It was always a traumatic crossing because the bed of the river was rocky and much afflicted with deep holes.

Lake Shala lady.

We seldom saw the locals but after we'd camped there several times the men and boys became relatively friendly. The women, still dressed in skins decorated with colourful beads, always passed in silence with wide, frightened eyes, or stood, obviously perplexed, gazing at us from a distance.

In the painting on the previous page, this lady of the lakes has grain in a pigskin bag. Her gourd will serve to hold milk or water or pulses. On her leg is a brass leg bangle which you can see in a photo (page 153) in the later story about Danakil. Round her neck, to keep her healthy, she wears an amulet holding spells inscribed on cow hide. Note her fine features. As a rule Ethiopians are not negroid.

Boys from a distant hamlet used to wade up and down the river's edges thrusting their spears into the reeds and, surprisingly, this apparently haphazard method caught tilapia which made excellent eating. The lads were happy to sell their catch but would accept only 5 cent coins. – They knew no other currency. On the far side of the lake the people were aware of only 10 cent coins; so we went camping with a bag full of the type of 'chicken feed' coins appropriate to the region where we planned to stay.

Remote folk on the shores of yet another lake hadn't registered that Haile Selassie was on the throne. They would only take old-fashioned, solid-silver Maria Theresa dollars. Being collector's pieces, they made buying local produce prohibitively expensive.

My brothers watched the fishing enviously, longing to have a go. The boys spent most of the time, in and out of the lake, wearing pyjamas which protected them from sunburn and which were comfortably loose in the heat. Soon bartering was in full swing. To fish Wyndham and Christopher needed a spear apiece, and the locals had been eyeing up the boys' 'pyjams'. It wasn't long before Wyndham had lost his PJ top in exchange for a fine spear. Grinning broadly he rushed off to shove his weapon into every promising bunch of reeds – with, alas (it has to be admitted) scant success! Christopher was having difficulty. He had a client willing to hand over a spear but the 'client' wanted his pyjama *trousers*, and Chris didn't quite like that idea. Bickering continued for some time; and the articles were traded again and again only for Christopher to change his mind each time and snatch back the preservers of his modesty.

At last the deed was done. Villager shot back home to show off his new finery; and, pulling down his pyjama top. Chris dashed

147

With his spear, Chris stands on one leg like the locals. He hasn't got third degree burns on his face. The pic is so old that stains can't be removed.

for the river. He didn't enjoy having his nether regions on display. Why he didn't revert to shorts or swimming trunks has never been established. Maybe he was too fixated on trying to spear fish. (Photos show that he and Wyndham were *sometimes* lucky!) Whatever the reason, he spent the next couple of days uncomfortably yanking his pyjama top down as far as it would go and looking miserable. Then the local guy decided he didn't think the pyjama pants were a fair swop and the deal was reversed. Chris read this account recently. He then told me:

"When I got them back my PJs smelled of smoky *toukul* fires and rancid butter ever after!"

Drama replaced farce when we realised that one of the car's tyres had gone flat. No problem: mending a puncture was pretty routine... We had tyre levers, a big hammer and stuff to patch inner tubes. If tyre levers and huge hammer didn't help to take the outer casing off the hub we knew how, with the spare tyre on, to drive over the punctured wheel and thus force the rubber away from the metal.

This time it wasn't difficult to get the inner tube out, but we discovered that the puncture was such a huge rent that we couldn't possibly mend it. A new inner tube would have to be bought – and that couldn't be done till we got home. We'd have to use the worn-thin spare wheel and hope like mad that we didn't have a puncture on the way home. One of the locals begged for the useless inner tube and, allowed to remove it, he was never seen again.

A tyre valve (and <u>small</u> matchstick for size.)

Consternation exploded when we put on the spare wheel and found that *that* was also flat! It was imperative to get the spare fixed. Repairing the second inner tube meant getting it free from its outer casing. To make this task less difficult it's valve was removed and then the air squeezed out of it. Zeleka scratched the inner's surface to make glue adhere and Father stuck a patch over the hole. Fine! Then we replaced the tube and inflated it. When it was time to re-insert the valve... the wretched thing had *vanished*! And the other had gone with the man who'd taken the previous very-split tube.

Pockets were searched and turned inside out. A valve was tiny and exactly the same colour as the pebbles. Horrors! Could the blessed thing have fallen into long grass? Ground and vegetation were carefully raked with anxious fingers and worried eyes for, without a device to stop air from rushing out of it, this tyre was useless. The tool kit contained no spare valve! The car therefore had only three useable wheels! It was at least 7 miles to walk through hot, prickly, animal-infested bush to the main 'road' and then goodness knew how many hours the walker would have to wait till anyone passed who could help with a valve (unlikely) or a lift to town.

We were stranded! A dreadful silence shrouded the tents. Gloom and despair engulfed everyone. Who would attempt the walk? Who would form the depleted group left to guard our belongings? How long till the guards were rescued? Would our food last out? The boys didn't mind not returning to school, and enjoyed the prospect of having more days in which to learn to fish... but our parents had to get back to work.

Miracles *do* happen. We kept on going back to where we'd been doing the repairs. Just as Dad finished packing essentials into a rucksack for a long, sweltering walk, Mother gave a delighted squeak! She'd found the lost valve. It was fitted. It worked!

Strained silence reigned all the way home; but amazingly the Land Rover managed to get back to Addis without having a puncture!

The Dreaded Danakil

The railway line, that climbs the horrendous escarpment from Djibuti (on the Red Sea) to Addis, was built with much difficulty partly because of terrible terrain, but mostly because it had to pass through Danakil territory. The Danakil were a famously-fearsome tribe with truly grisly customs. A young man couldn't marry till he had enough dried human testicles strung round his neck. To obtain such trophies raids on other villages were carried out with great cruelty, and abducted females were subjected to awful treatment. Their men brandished fantastic, curved knives suitable for slicing off genitals, and the women loved jewellery made from copper stolen from telephone lines. (Pic of telephonewire bracelet is on page 153.)

Awash Station on the railway line was within Danakil country but this didn't daunt my parents when they decided to visit a just-declared game reserve and a hot spring near the Awash Station. Into the Land Rover we clattered – without our faithful Zeleka this time as, with a slight nod of recognition to the dangerous region, we planned to use the tiny station's *albergo* (primitive hotel) instead of tents.

Trying to make as little disturbance as possible, so as not to attract attention of hostile tribes-people in the region, we bumped through sparse Acacia woodland and tufts of Cactus. The puncture happened when we had made good progress into the bush. For a great many miles we had been struggling through a totally deserted landscape when pphfffsh ! bump! bump! – the rear left tyre went flat. Peering round fearfully, we pulled off the ridiculous square 'cushion' that was provided as the driver's seat in those days. Under that was a metal sheet which had to be removed to let us find a small space where tools were stored.

We changed the wheel. Had any Danakil seen our predicament? So far no-one had approached. Sighs of relief changed to gasps of horror as we realised that the 'new' tyre was dangerously low. It wasn't exactly flat but it needed a good dose of air. The pump was extracted from the tool box and attached to the engine. Then we waited anxiously for the tyre to fill. It took *ages*! But still no Danakil flourishing spears, machetes and terrifying knives appeared. It became possible to detach the pump. Again sighs of relief circulated below the surrounding Acacias.

Danakil youth with a short spear and a regulation, notorious, angled, Danakil knife – just dandy for castrating your enemy – or even your friend if you're short of a pair of testicles. Often a man carried a dagger as well.

Then TERROR! Through the trees we spotted a posse of Ethiopians marching purposefully towards us from our rear. They'd had just enough time to observe our problem and collect into a gang! "Get into the car!" ordered Father.

"Quickly" added Mother.

We obeyed with great alacrity. There was petrified silence. But what was Dad *doing*? Instead of throwing the pump and its leads into the back of the car with all possible speed, and replacing the 'cushion' 'any old how' to leap into the driving seat and carry us away from the approaching aggressors as fast as the terrain would allow... instead of forcing the old car to its (slow) maximum speed... he was bent over the stupid tool box, and painfully slowly winding the pump lead back into place!

"Come on" urged Mother frantically. But he silently finished his job, fastidiously replaced the metal, then the 'cushion' and was

about to slowly climb into the driver's seat. Later he said:
"Mustn't let them see you're rattled!"

My Goodness! What *sang froid*! The rest of us were sitting frozen with fear. In horrified silence, heads down, eyes on the floor, almost too frightened to breathe, we just waited to be slaughtered – or worse.

In those days young people were not as informed as they are in the 21st century. I suspected vaguely what happened to the *male* victims of Danakil warriors but the word 'rape' wasn't in my vocabulary. I had no idea of the ghastly things that 'bad men' did to women; but from shocked whispers of adults I knew that the deeds were appalling and agonising. This ignorance helped me to be brave. It also liberated my mind to all sorts of nightmarish ideas. What were these terrible Danakil about to inflict upon us? I was deeply troubled for my brothers and father; and, terrified that it would be done in full view, I was almost out of my mind with embarrassment and dread of their pain. As for my mother and me – I was so petrified that I couldn't even *begin* to react.

My brothers, though much younger, had a very good grasp of how the Danakil treated their victims. Wilfred Thesiger, famous explorer of The Iraqi Marshes, The Empty Quarter and of other desolate desert regions, had taken them shooting and had not spared *any* details. At the time it had seemed titillating. Now they wished they did *not* know how the Danakil behaved.

Meanwhile the group of wild-looking fellows advanced. They reached the Land Rover. And then, miraculously, they parted. Some went by on the left and others marched past on the right. Were they planning to attack from all round? Christopher, not really old enough to credit what might be about to overtake us, watched them and smiled through the window. He told us afterwards that one of the men had smiled back.

Father was poised, apparently innocuously, outside the vehicle, but clutching a tyre lever, ready to do battle. Even he was 'paralysed' with gratitude to the Powers Above as the group hurried off into the trees. We gaped in silent disbelief.

Later, thinking about those terrible moments, we decided that the Danakil hadn't been a warring party. They had had with them women and children. Maybe they had just been 'going places' and were not in the mood to kill and take trophies. Whatever...! That was a *very* close call! In fact, so scaring had the episode been that, after enjoying (always with one eye out for possible attack) the completely unpopulated Hot Springs, Mother refused to risk the family again. She insisted on returning by train – and that opened up still more adventures.

We waited till a locomotive struggled to arrive from Djibouti. With the maximum of shouting and excitement, railway workers pushed the Land Rover up *steeply* inclined planks from the railway line to the platform of a flatbed truck which was luckily discovered in a siding. Our car was lashed to the carriage with a spider's web of ropes and we were invited to sit inside.

"Do not get out of your vehicle" we were told – an order that we immediately disregarded! As we chugged up through magnificent scenery it was tremendous fun to be able to walk about on the wooden platform way up high above trees, bushes and boulders, and to gasp at spectacular mountain scenery.

Our goods train clattered round the rim of a volcano that, in geological parlance, is extremely young. It was so recent that no vegetation had had time to start a foothold. Great black solidified eruptions, like boiling boulders from Hades, covered the vast cup which was then called 'the Garibaldi Crater'. Ethiopia has other volcanoes which, unlike this one, are still active. On another trip we had the harrowing experience of arriving just as a bush pig underwent its last throes of drowning in a pool of steaming, simmering tar. That left an indelible scar on the memory. Away from the solidified black lava we saw much game, and cameras went wild. In due course our train rolled into Nazareth Station and, with the usual yells and palaver, our car was lowered from its vantage site. It seemed awfully

dull driving back to Addis at ground level!

Leg bangles, made from stolen brass or copper, were favoured by Lakes ladies and by Danakil ladies alike. I bought these for empty tins and/or salt and/or sugar. The one at the top right here is on the leg of the skin-clad Shala lady in the painting (page 146).

153

Stranded men of God

The road from Diredawa to Harar used to negotiate a big wadi. Vehicles had to scramble down one side of the ravine, follow the floor of the usually-dry, bouldery river for some distance and then struggle up the far side of the small gorge. It was a very hot part of Ethiopia so a couple of priests decided to disrobe while they travelled along the deserted track.

As their vehicle bounced over the atrocious stretch of 'road' between cliffs and along the river bed they heard an ominous rumble. Rain up in the mountains had caused a bore to sweep down the wadi. Terrified rearwards glances showed them a heart-stoppingly huge wall of boiling water and spinning rocks chasing towards them. Leaping out of their Land Rover they scuttled to the cliffside. Their vehicle disappeared, tumbling over and over, engulfed in a maelstrom of great trees, drowning creatures, bodies of wild animals, and other debris... all swept away by the violent torrent. Clambering desperately, battered, nearly overcome by the rapidly-moving, muddy flood, they managed to reach rocks where they clung, and then perched, till the deluge had subsided.

Then they gazed at each other in horror! Caked in grime and wearing nothing but filthy Y-fronts, they had many miles to go till they reached their Mission. That was in the days before mobile phones, and anyway, they were in the back of beyond where there would have been no cover.

Devoutly thanking God for their delivery, they set their faces to the road, and prayed that no transport from their sister nunnery would be the first vehicle – if any – to eventually pass.

This Monitor Lizard had succumbed to the flood.

154

Marooned on Nightmare Island.

Our camp at Lake Langano

One dreadful day I was marooned on a rocky islet in Lake Langano. I'm told that the region is now a popular holiday resort with hotels boasting all mod cons. In my day it was still beautifully deserted except for the occasional weekend camping party.

On the far shore, and opposite to our tents, there seemed to be a peninsular and, as we had chosen a site near to the end of the vast pinkish-brown expanse, Fritz, Harry and I decided to walk round to investigate. Harry soon caught his swimsuit on a thorn. There was a tearing sound as a triangle of bright blue came adrift. Whiskers, of course, was fascinated by this flapping brightness and jumped to seize it. In those day men's swimsuits were tight – no boxer shorts even dreamt of – so – after a much louder rip and a yell from Harry, – Fritz and I collapsed laughing. A large expanse of the victim's 'cheek' was exposed to the baking sun, and Whiskers was scampering up an Acacia tree clutching a bright blue prize. Later I bought Harry a new swimsuit but for the rest of that weekend he went about 'half-nude'. Regions that should never have been exposed became painfully sunburnt!

Tramping through the scrub we found that it was much further round the head of the lake than we had expected; but eventually, hot and tired, yet triumphant, we were near the mysterious 'peninsular'. Crikey! It wasn't a peninsular – it was an island. How exciting! Pythons were known to enjoy islands.

'It'd be fun,' we thought, 'to wander carefully round the islet and look for them.' (We must have been daft! Pythons could be seen *anywhere*!) But we knew we'd never get to the island. Apart from the fear of crocs, the width of murky waters was probably too wide for us to swim. Frustrated, we gazed at the distant trees and rocks and wished we could get across.

A raft of sorts was lying on the pebbly, grey shore so we wondered if we might be able to punt over. As we approached the rickety contraption, its spear-flourishing owner appeared out of reeds to protect his belongings, and after a good deal of explanatory pantomime, and persuasion he grudgingly agreed to take us across the 'strait'.

The very primitive 'craft' was obviously not capable of supporting more than one of us at a time so, very 'gallantly' the men immediately decided that it should be a case of 'ladies first'.

"You test it out," they said cheerfully. "If it collapses we'll attempt a rescue before the crocs get you."

Whiskers had already made a thorough inspection of the roughly-tied branches; but although he disapproved of the ramshackle thing, when it was pushed onto the water, he wasn't going to be left behind so, sitting on my shoulder, he clung tightly to my head and chattered disapprovingly. Looking equally miserable, Coneetcha balanced as best she could, while little by little we floundered across and were deposited on the rocky lump.

We had expected the 'boat' man to return for Fritz and Harry and then, a little later, to raft as back to the mainland. But, having dumped me, he took off down the coast, ignoring the shouts of us three '*ferengis*'. Obviously he considered that the men had wanted to be rid of a troublesome female and were now cheering with delight. Perhaps he even decided he had achieved a brotherly humanitarian success. Be that as it may I was inescapably marooned.

If she hadn't ended up as a tasty croc mouthful, the dog would probably have slowly made the crossing back; and on my own I might have managed to risk the reptiles and swim the brown stretch; but hampered with a monkey desperate not to fall off, scratching at my bare back with his sharp claws, I'd never reach the shore.

The raft man vanished. I imagined pythons toughening their coils behind me and wriggling out from every nook and cranny in the boulders. Fritz yelled. Harry yelled. I yelled. In vain! Our waterman had evanesced! Back in camp we had no boat.

"We're going to hunt for a village," shouted my friends and abandoning me, they disappeared into the bush. It was dreadfully lonely and spooky alone on that wisp of island. In the silence, across the channel sundry animals came down to drink. I jumped every time a twig crackled. Coneetcha wasn't happy. She made the atmosphere twice as desperate by staying glued to my shins and whining miserably. I watched herons, kingfishers, eagles... and thought jealously that they could fly *anywhere* – even across watery expanses. Whiskers regained his courage and leapt about the trees eating Acacia pods which made him smell foul. My patch of shade moved round. I was frightened and hungry. The men didn't re-appear. Would I have to sleep here? How many days till my friends got hold of a boat? Would they have to go to Addis to find one?

Eventually a small figure, fighting a raft, appeared very far away. Fritz was doing his unstable best to flounder in my direction. Finding the craft on shore and unguarded, the men had 'stolen' it. Inexpertly we used it, and left it, with no regrets, on the beach, before plodding wearily back to camp extremely late and very exhausted.

"At one point we spotted you through the binoculars," said the three who had spent a lazy day in camp. "You seemed to be having a lot of fun walking on water. How did you manage that?"

Fun! HUH!

A case of curious biology.

In a greatly perturbed state Ato Woobie burst into the Head's office. "They are cutting the trees off Mr Wingard's backside!" he yelled indignantly. My bemused father probed delicately for elucidation. Ato Woobie, it seemed, had seen strangers chopping down blue gums in the empty land behind the Wingards' bungalow.

157

Exam panache

Frank Dawson, who is mentioned in the next story, had – amongst other matters – taught his younger pupils about methods of transport. In the end-of-term exam one of his questions asked:
"How would you get to, and what crops would you expect to see, if you went to: Lalibela, Asmara, Jimma?"
On his answer sheet one logical, bright spark wrote:
"But, Mr Dawson, I don't <u>want</u> to go to those places!"

Blue Nile Bandits

{NOTES:
Shifta (bandits) were a constant threat on roads out of town. They made barriers or otherwise stopped travellers. Then they stole EVERYTHING, including clothes, and left the travellers naked – and usually dead – by the roadside.}

The Blue Nile – or the Abaie as it is known locally – flows southwards out of Lake Tana in Ethiopia. Then it bends gradually round in a clockwise sense to eventually pour north and join the White Nile near Khartoum. At first, apart from a bouldery stretch, it flows tranquilly for about 20 miles across a broad plain: a modest river in the dry season but a wide, turbulent flood during the Rains. Everything changes when – suddenly – dramatically – it throws itself, hissing and roaring, splashing prodigiously, over an abyss. These are the Tisesat Falls – a wonderfully onomatopoeic name.

Here clouds of boiling spray spew high into the sky. It's strangely like a version of the Victoria Falls, and it's no surprise that local tribes call them: 'The Smoke that Thunders' (VF) and 'The Big Smoke' (TF). After the Tisesat Falls the Blue Nile crashes down in a series of tremendous gorges with sides so steep and deep that, until recently, they were unvisited by humans, and even wild animals could get down to drink only at rare places.

When my family lived in Ethiopia, because of the threat posed by the notorious *Shifta*, many people refused to leave the 'security' of Addis, or of lesser towns. My parents were different. There was all that *immensity* of truly spectacular scenery waiting to be appreciated... When possible we loaded the long-suffering car with our primitive camping gear and set out exploring, over *terrible* 'tracks' and across bridges that were often fearfully rickety or even totally collapsed.

Friends were appalled when they learnt that we proposed to drive to the only place where a road reached, and crossed, the Blue Nile, and to camp in the Abaie gorge. They were convinced that *Shifta* would do their worst. But, one weekend, ignoring pleas to abandon the plan, frightened but excited, we climbed into the Austin. – What that vehicle achieved before we acquired a Land Rover is hard to believe.

By the standards of the day the road to the canyon was good dirt so, after only a few hours, we reached the place where the silvery, gravel track disappeared over a steep edge. We couldn't see the river, a mile below, and we'd have to travel many tortuous miles before we got to it. The other side was 15 miles away, and in between that and us were precipices and ordinary drops interspersed with small plateaux. The narrow thread of primitive road wound down and down and down, passing through different vegetations which depended upon the climates of the various altitudes.

Cautiously, wary of potholes and crumbling roadsides, we nudged the vehicle down hairpin bends. Lining the route to watch this unusual spectacle, urchins from a lonely hamlet, scattered nimbly away from the edge when we had to go forwards and backwards to get round one of the many tight turns. They'd seen what happened to trucks whose brakes had failed and didn't want to be in the way!

We found a small plateau about half way down, pitched camp and, due to the lack of inhabitants here, had no trouble finding wood for a splendid fire. All was going marvellously... Suddenly we heard the rumble of a heavy vehicle. Pricking the darkness its headlights appeared and vanished as it negotiated bends above us. PANIC! Steadily it dropped nearer and nearer. We realised how stupid we'd been, not only to venture into known *Shifta* territory, but also to publicise our presence with the fire, and songs. Our descent had been noticed and this was prime hold-up terrain. Terrified, we looked round for places in which to hide, but short of jumping off the cliff, there wasn't much scope for that. We picked up stones.

The lorry growled down and – Horrors! – it turned off the road onto our little plateau! It parked alongside our car. By the light of the fire we saw that it was jam-packed full of Ethiopian men. They had rifles and spears. Our last hour had arrived! There was nothing to be done but to brazen it out and hope for the best. Of course we'd fight tooth a nail but what could we do against such a horde of burly ruffians? Two fellows clambered out of the truck and advanced towards us. My father moved in front of the family: a futile attempt to protect us. Our knees turned to jelly. I felt my tongue stick to the roof of my mouth.

Then one of the dark figures said: "Good evening Mrs. Heyring."

John Tiffin and Frank Dawson, colleagues of my mother at The General Wingate Secondary School for Ethiopian boys, had obtained permission from the Ministry of Education to take their Sixth Form pupils, with a bodyguard of armed soldiers, on a Geography trip to the Abaie gorge! We nearly passed out with relief (!), and enjoyed a marvellous weekend together revelling in the breath-taking views of that incredible canyon.

The rhyme below (Abaie Shifta) is fun if sung to the tune of "The Island."

{The Island: - (Traditional).

1ˢᵗ verse   *Chorus:*
Daddy Neptune, one da-ay,   *Oh what a snug little island,*
to Neptune did sa-ay: *A right little, tight little island.*
"If ever I lived upon dry land,   *All the world round,*
the place I would hit on   *none can be found*
would be little Britain"   *so happy as this little island.}*
Said Freedom:
"Why that's my own island."   The tune can be found on the internet.

Abaie SHIFTA!

We were planning one da-ay
to camp at Abaie – aie,
but friends said: "Beware of the Shifta!
They're beasty and bad
and you'll surely be sad
if you're caught by the blood-curdling Shifta!

> CHORUS: (*con brio*) Oh what a jolly old prospect!
> To find by the Shifta our path checked –
> Shifta galore!
> SHRRRRRRRRIEEEKING for gore!
> Our corpses and goods their sole ob-ject.

Persevering however
we got there – and never
had even the whiff of a Shifta.
The tents were put u –up...
We'd started to su-up...
The camp fire was all of a-glitter.

CHORUS: (*Languidly*) ------   Oh - what a weird invention
to say we would get a 'reception'!
We were at ease
munching our cheese
and no one gave Shifta a mention.

Then tranquillity shattered!
towards us there clattered
a lorry – which stopped right beside us!
A truck full of cro-oks
with TERRIBLE lo-oks!
The Shifta had followed and found us!

CHORUS: *(terrified)* Oh what a spine-chilling moment!
We froze! Much too shocked for a movement.
There we just stood –
eyed by that brood –
who leapt from their lorry to torment.

In our shoes we were shaking.
Our knees they were quaking,
as some of them marched to our clearing...
Then one of them said:
"Good ev'ning to you, Mrs Heyring."

CHORUS: (*cheerfully and loudly:*)
Oh what relief and amazement
to find them a Wingate contingent!
Geography mad,
Frank and Tiff had
brought them by special arrangement.

A brave, foolhardy and historic deed

In 1961 I camped with friends, right beside the Abaie River. So that guards on the bridge wouldn't see us we rose before dawn, and Arne Rubin (a Swedish dentist) set off in a kayak down the Blue Nile. *No-one had ever before managed to navigate the mysterious flow.* Our hearts were in our mouths for we thought we'd seen the last ever of our mad friend who, sharing our fears, hadn't dared to tell his wife of his plans. He asked us to inform her of his actions. Against all odds, 2 weeks later Arne turned up at Khartoum!

I don't think he ever got the fame he deserved.

The following is the *last* 'poem' – I promise you!
It commemorates our camp beside the mystic Blue Nile.

ABAIE

Where the gorge is wide, so wide across that details disappear,
and the crags upon the other side thrust amber, hot and sheer –
past the final mud-thatch village, where the daily drummers play,
we drop sharply off the plateau leaving peaks remote and grey.
    Scarcely there, the wisp of 'silver', hugging contours steep – or mild –
    plunges dusty into territory beautiful and wild.
Braving hours of bumping miles, unfurling bends and views that thrill,
we attain the inmost valley glow'ring empty, low and still.
Both its sides are steep and stony, yet a complement of trees
wrests a roothold round the cliff-edge, in the crevices and screes.
 – Not a sign of habitation – not a human, or a cow –
just the lonely throb of silence as convecting breezes sough.
    Here the river ripples gently over boulders blanched and black,
    shallows swiftly to the pattern of its broad and languid track.
    In the distance, with his egret, basks the gaping crocodile,
    as small pipers, all unconscious, roam the sandbanks of the Nile.

While the noonday thermals shimmer we lie idle in the shade,
dozing gently, talking softly, till the heat begins to fade.
Then the tents are quickly mounted – tiny objects – hardly seen
on the rough floor of the valley, where long pythons hide, serene.
    At the water's edge we wallow, finding driftwood for the fire,
    wander up and down the shingle till our lazy footfalls tire.
    Then we sit and watch the monkeys as they gambol on the shore –
    mock a cheeky babe who's punished and then goes and asks for more!

162

Wise baboons sedately stepping in their class-determined file
saunter down to sup the waters of the sunset-tinted Nile.
Massive Grandpa, at the rearguard, barks his orders, and defies
any leopard who is lurking with intention in her eyes.
>   Lewdly jibes the coarse hyena just emerging from his lair
>   and his weird warble oscillates mysterious, dark'ning air.
>   But in spite of him small duikers, eyes and ears a-twitch with fright...
>   will flit caref'lly to the river, drink, and, soundless, melt from sight.

Through   long,   rustly   hours   of   indigo,   more cautious shades will creep
over pebbles, down dry gullies – where the starlight tries to seep,
frisk their tails towards the heavens, sink their furry jowls to drink,
flick off coloured drops like gemstones as they pause there on the brink:
>   heterogeneous procession: serval, porcupine and fox,
>   wily jackal whistling echoes off the quickly-cooling rocks.
From the hares and fluffy hyrax; from the night-apes, cats and owls
there'll be scuffles in the darkness, squeaks and coughing, grunts and howls.

And we'll lie there under canvas, till a secret sound or cry
filters – strangely – through Acacia (swaying black against the sky).
Then we'll lose our bedroll drowsiness...   We'll peer through slitted door,
shine the torch, to catch a glimmer –
>   and

>   – tomorrow –

>   find the spoor.

- - - - - - - - - - - -

Nappies?

    The teachers at The General Wingate School were fond of tennis. On Sunday mornings small fry played outside the courts while their parents competed, serving, smashing and shouting with verve. Mr Marshall, the Maths teacher, and energetic Scottish Dancer, had a pair of snazzy, brief tennis shorts made of white towelling.

    One day a notable sportsman, visiting from the UK, had been persuaded to umpire a tensely-anticipated Wingate-versus-Embassy match. A large crowd collected to watch. In the awed and reverent silence that reigned as the visitor was ushered onto the court a piercing cry came from my infant brother, Wyndham:
"Mummy, why is Mr Marshall wearing a nappy?"

Leaping Tommy

My brothers and I used to ride about 8km to school. It was possible to canter comfortably along an expanse of mud that stretched beside the narrow tar of the 'highway'; but we had to rein in at regular intervals where deep, wide culverts (made beneath the potholed macadam) allowed heavy rainfall to drain away as streams.

One morning a herd of the usual little humped cows, en route to market, was coming under the road through a temporarily dry culvert just as we approached it. Chris, the horse-boy and I slowed, and stopped on the side of the drain to let the cows pass. But, in the lead, Wyndham and his mount – Tommy – got the shock of their lives!

Tommy was a good little jumper so when he found his way blocked by pesky cattle passing below him, he simply leapt over the annoying beasts, and landed on the far side of the gully. It was the funniest sight I'd seen in a long time. The cows, as startled to have a flying horse whizzing above them as we were to watch the event, tossed their long horns and rolled frightened eyes.

Never before had Tommy (or Wyndham) flown so high or so far! Amazingly they landed safely but both were wide-eyed, puffing and trembling. The rest of us just laughed with relief and surprise till the tears rolled down our cheeks.

Two Oxpeckers between the horns of the dozing cow have just enjoyed a good meal by picking ticks off her.

Dicing with Death

It's always a sin to acquire wild animals. To do so only encourages cruel traders; but when my mother saw a tiny Grivet Monkey being hauled about by two urchins in the market, she knew it was near death. It needed food, love and warmth. Giving the boys a few coins she brought the little beast home, to die – she thought – in peace. He didn't die. He thrived. Even then, as a wee baby, he had magnificent white whiskers growing elegantly up and backwards from each side of his little black face. So he became 'Whiskers'.

The Grivet was still very young when (to Whiskers' teasing delight) Coneetcha joined the family, and it was many years before she learnt that she was a dog and not a monkey. If we were out riding her frustration was ludicrous when she couldn't copy her preceptor, as he jumped onto my shoulder. Often he raced up trees but when she tried to emulate his nimble swings, poor Coneetcha landed with a bump, and was left standing perplexed at the base of the trunk.

Until he was strong enough to graduate into the garden, Whiskers lived in a pouch on my chest, and gradually made increasingly bold forays into the outside world. If I was outside he was left loose and often created mayhem among the chickens, tortoises and rabbits, but unless supervised, he was so mischievous that he was given a belt with a light chain that slid along a very lengthy run-wire. It stretched right across the paddock. From his bedroom, a box high on the wall of the stables, he could jump down onto the horses, groom their manes, and pull their ears. It was a miracle that his chain didn't become entangled in poles, branches and the fence over which he scrambled with cheeky delight.

Just once he nearly snuffed it. I found him hanging upside down, wound up in his chain like a fly twisted into a spider's web. His eyes were popping. His eyelids, always baby-blue with powder-blue edges, were tightly closed giving a weird effect of 'already dead'. His tongue was sticking out; but despite his critical state, as I started to desperately unravel the chain from his little body, he sighed faintly: "Grok! Grook!" which is what he used to say when he was happy. Then, as breath began to return, even before he was well enough to open his eyes, again he told me: "Grok! Grook!"
His gratitude brought tears to my eyes.

165

He revived amazingly quickly but seemed to have hurt his instep rather badly so after a day and a half of watching him jump, slip and fall (so utterly unlike him) I took him to the vet. The foot was only very badly bruised and in few days he was using it again normally. Would that humans recovered so quickly!

After that his run was changed and we never had any recurrences of that terrible event – an 'excitement' I could well have done without.

Another 'excitement' that was almost a tragedy.

Teachers of The General Wingate School challenged The British Embassy Staff to see which establishment could win the most points at a swimming gala. The response was robust; so one Friday evening cars convened at Ambo, a small place about an hour's drive west of Addis. There, behind a notice which said: "Bathing costumes are compulsory", an entrepreneur had excavated a *vast*, roughly-rectangular hole from the mountainside. It formed a huge and extremely-deep pool which was filled by springs that poured out from rocks, providing water hot enough to simmer peas. Mind you – we never did use that water for cooking. It was so sulphurous that the food would have been inedible. Luckily the pool's surface area was so enormous that a lot of heat was lost to the atmosphere and no-one got more than *par*-boiled.

Races took place on Saturday but on Friday evening, with tents erected beside the pool, and supper eaten, an energetic game of Water Polo caused much excitement. As very hot water splashed into cold night air the pool was completely engulfed in swirling steam; and strange, yellow floodlights produced a Dante-esque scene. Bodies appeared to writhe beneath ominous, rolling, ochre clouds. It was almost impossible to see other swimmers – which made it tricky when deciding where to throw the ball! – and the chaotic match might have come out of 'Alice Through the Looking Glass'.

Zeleka watched it all with great interest and presumably concluded that the sides of the pool shelved, like the edges of the Lakes. He approached the water. If all those *ferengis* (foreigners) could disport themselves in the lovely hot bath, then so would *he*! Boldly stepping onto the surface he was amazed to find himself, not walking *on* it, but rapidly sinking into deep, sulphurous depths.

Luckily for Zeleka, Mother had spotted his advance. In two ticks she had dived in where the servant had disappeared. The water was so murky and the steam so thick that there was absolutely no chance of seeing a sinking body, but fortunately her searching hands felt his poll; so, grabbing a fistful of fuzzy hair, she extracted him, choking and spluttering, from the water.

An inflated inner tube was procured for Zeleka's use for the rest of the weekend, and he had strict instructions to tell someone if he planned to immerse himself again. Despite his fright he had a great time that weekend – almost as wonderful as the hours he spent later telling his Addis friends about his exploits!

Capital punishment.

Linking Addis with the surrounding countryside were many market 'roads'. These were wide and usually passable by trucks but they had not been built for the movement of vehicles. Over time they'd been beaten into existence by the passage of thousands of plodding hoofs of cattle coming in to market or to the slaughterhouse, and also by thousands of clip-clopping little hoofs of small donkeys carrying huge loads of all types of produce such as hay, wood, empty cans, chaff (to be used to bind mud in making *toukul* walls)... all to be sold in the Big Market. Bare feet of equally-laden humans and of cattle- and donkey- drovers, did their share at smoothing the surfaces of the market 'roads'.

In the Entoto mountain range behind our home there was a particularly wide and pleasant track that gave magnificent 360° views across expanses of rolling plains. My brother Wyndham, and I, with the *syce* (groom), rode up to the ridge one beautiful day. Young blue gums sparkled in sunshine that was pouring over everything. The sky was a deep, high-altitude ultramarine and the air was crisp. The road was seething with the usual bustle of country folk coming into town or returning to their distant villages; but near the coll swirled a small, stationary crowd. As we headed towards the excited rabble I got a terrible shock.

Suddenly we saw that the people were pressing round a big truck. In the back was a man with a noose round his neck. The other end of the rope was attached to a crossbar tied between two upright eucalyptus poles. This was a gibbet. The truck was about to be driven off so the wretched prisoner would be yanked off the back of the vehicle and left hanging and jerking from the gallows.

Hangings were a fact of life in those days. Condemned criminals were 'saved up' until the authorities had enough of them to string up at least one on each of many market 'roads,' as well as in the Horse Market, the Big Market and elsewhere. Most little boys attended Priests' schools, sitting on the ground in big circles under shade trees and chanting scripture to the skies. It was thought beneficial for Priests to take their pupils to watch hangings. Certainly after these public punishments the crime rate dropped dramatically.

Children sit on the ground round a central cleric at a Priest's school.

Our *syce* thought it was a great joke and a huge piece of luck that we should have hit upon the gruesome event at absolutely the precise moment of drama. Probably he had known all along that we were heading towards the scene of action. But Wyndham and I were shattered to the core. We turned our horses and shot off home as fast as they would take us.

Apart from blurting out why we had returned so early the matter was never again mentioned so I don't know whether it affected my brother; but for years afterwards I suffered intermittently from nightmares, waking gasping for breath and feeling that a noose was strangling me. After hangings we took particular care not to go near the sites of gallows till weeks later when it was safe to assume that enough time had passed for the bodies to have been removed.

168

Thank you Professor Pasteur

On January 22nd the family was at lunch when geese in the back garden set up a terrible racket. I went to investigate. As I emerged from the kitchen door a dog, rushed up and bit me. Luckily it didn't continue into the house but galloped frenziedly out of the garden.

The wound wasn't deep but the entire family was terrified. The biter had been frothing at the mouth. That and its weird behaviour told us that the poor creature was obviously suffering from rabies. But it had attacked through my jodhpurs so we all hoped that any toxin might have been wiped off. Nevertheless, we hurried to the Pasteur Institute where our illusions were immediately dashed.

"She has to have anti-rabies injections," declared a doctor.

"But" said Father, "she's taking a scholarship exam on Feb 10th."

"If you'd ever seen anyone die of rabies you wouldn't hesitate for a second," replied the medic sombrely. "She *has* to have the injections. Rabies is a ghastly death."

So for the next *twenty one* days I attended the Institute to have a daily dose of 5 cc of anti-rabies vaccine injected into my tummy. 5 ml is a *large* quantity and the stuff, which was thickish, had to be injected slowly using what seemed to be an *enormous* syringe. The treatment was a daily horror. By Feb 12th – the end of the 3 weeks – I had so many punctures and bruises that it was hard to locate a place where the needle could be thrust. But thanks to Dr Louis Pasteur I survived.

To reach Britain in time my exam answers went by Diplomatic Bag. Then I was invited by telegram to attend for interview. Mrs Sandford cabled her daughter, Audrey: "Daphne Heyring (13) arriving Victoria Air Terminal 10 pm Feb 16th. Please meet and retain." Poor Audrey hadn't a clue who 'Daphne' was!

My only warm clothes with which to face the British winter were 2 old, white, vyella blouses. Mother ran up some woollen pyjamas and lent me a well-worn grey skirt and a yellow cardigan. Mrs Nutman lent me a beige coat. With that 'vast' (!) wardrobe – of colours, that did *nothing* for my complexion – I landed in the UK in the worst pea-soup smog of the season. For 2 hours I sat wondering, but with an African's patience, in the imposing, at-that-hour-empty terminal. Audrey and husband arrived at midnight after the devil of a trip up from Surrey. They had driven straight *over* a roundabout.

169

In my borrowed 'finery' I passed the interview and spent 5 very happy years at Wycombe Abbey School.

Decades later I was again exposed to rabies. This time so much progress had been made that I had only 6 smallish injections. Nowadays (2018) only 4 jabs are needed – given over 14 days.

When incredulous friends hear of my brushes with hydrophobia they think it's highly amusing to say: "Well, that explains a lot!"

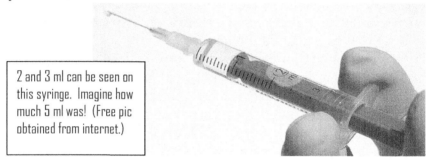

2 and 3 ml can be seen on this syringe. Imagine how much 5 ml was! (Free pic obtained from internet.)

How to foil malign Spirits

During the Rains the usually fordable Sebilo Stream en route to the Sandfords' farm, became a fast, swirling river, impassable to cars. We then rode horses to the farm. Humans, saddles and luggage crossed the Sebilo on a 2-man raft (made of planks tied over barrels) which was hauled across with ropes. Our steeds were likewise pulled over. Some horses happily belly-flopped off the bank and relished the swim. Others had to be pushed. Snorting, they all swam with bared teeth, raised tails and much splashing. We had to stand well clear as they enjoyed a magnificent shake on reaching the further bank.

When a bridge was eventually built the locals were adamant that the Rains would wash it away unless a black goat was sacrificed to the Water Spirit. The Sandfords, being good Christians, ignored this suggestion; and during the first three Rainy Seasons, the arches duly disintegrated – often. They were rebuilt – again and *again*.

Everyone was careful not to comment on a mysterious red stain that appeared on the fifth bridge after a particularly dark, moonless night. This crossing lasted for decades. Carefully concealed in the farm foreman's accounts was a strange entry: "Black Goat"!

The bath plug

Mr Peel, the British Consul who featured in the story about the attempted *Coup d'Etat*, was travelling with his Ambassador round Ethiopia to 'show the flag'. In convoy with their Land Rover they had a three-ton lorry carrying *a lot* of camping gear and many servants. In the back of the truck were two 44-gallon drums full of fuel for the vehicles, and two more barrels with the same quantity of water. But with all that luggage they missed one essential.

One night they didn't have to camp. They were invited to use a 'fine' rest house that had *two* (!) bathrooms! Mr Peel was slightly perturbed to find that there was no key to any door but, banishing such a minor trouble from his mind, he had, with a satisfied sigh, just sunk into his warm tub, and was relishing the chance to rid himself of the dirt and sweat of a hard day on the road, when his bathroom door burst open. In rushed the Ambassador's valet. The fellow plunged his arm into Mr Peel's water and, without any 'By your leave', extracted the bath plug. Muttering: "H.E. wants a bath," he dashed out again.

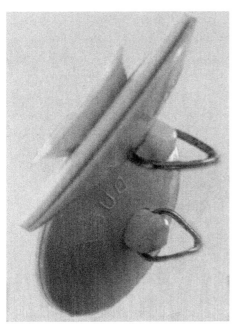

It transpired that although the establishment had two bath *rooms* it had only one bath *plug*! To avoid being stranded cold and damp, the poor Consul had to insert his heel into the outlet of the bath: a method that he discovered was not only painful but also inefficient.

It's strange how bath plugs seem to go A.W.O.L. Even in developed countries I always have a fit-all-holes plug in my toilet bag, and it has come in handy times beyond counting. It was last used by a group of us staying in a small hotel in the Spanish Pyrenees. After a week of tramping about the heights we were extraordinarily muddy and disgustingly sweaty. But although our simple accommodation boasted three bathrooms it had not a single plug! That provided a good excuse to hammer on doors, and also to have another beer while waiting for my fit-all plug to become available.

The 'fit-all-drains' plug shown on the previous page has been placed on a mirror so that both its top and bottom surfaces can be seen.

<u>Sorry – No toilet paper.</u>

There are establishments in the developed world which complain because they aren't given a few million to build a new wing. Others want to refurbish already splendid laboratories, or say they can't do without extra facilities for deprived children.

'Deprived' is a relative term. In Addis *real* deprivation was all round us; and it's sad to recount that although it made our hearts bleed, we just learnt to accept awful sights and the appalling conditions in which some humans existed. I hope things are completely different nowadays, but in the 1960s wandering the streets outside the school were hideously maimed lepers; and some adults and children with useless, contorted limbs, whose only means of getting about was to crouch on a home-cobbled contraption on little wheels – and they were the 'lucky' ones whose families had somehow scratched together the funds to buy the wheels and planks. Others simply had to rely on weak relatives to carry them to spots where they sat all day to beg.

scar where ice has refrozen after wire sank thru' melt water

ice

Copper wire

2kg 6kg 3kg

Regelation experiment
[Method of supporting the ice is not shown.]

Our school labs were adequately equipped and some of our pupils came from well-to-do families. Yet when I took a block of ice to school to demonstrate a simple regelation experiment it caused a *sensation*! I put the ice on the ground-floor veranda outside the lab so that the melt water could dribble away into the garden, and also so that students could pop by all morning to watch the progress of weighted wires passing through the ice, which reformed once the wire had sunk through that level. The girls had no conception of ice. This was the first time they'd seen it. There were loud exclamations from the crowd (of pupils and grounds-men and even of fascinated Ethiopian teachers) that congregated. Brave fingers were extended to touch the weird substance.

But we really knew the meaning of 'Not enough money' when we weren't paid... Every month the entire staff from Mrs Varghese the Indian Director, in her magnificent saris, to Hundi the humble lad who swept the drive, were summoned to the Staffroom where we stood in an expectant line to have our names called out by a couple of men from The Ministry of Education. They sat at the table with ledgers and little bags of money. When your name was carefully read aloud from a list you approached and had the appropriate notes and coins counted out. You signed – or had your fingerprint taken, according to whether or not you could write – and went back to work. In Europe it would be unthinkable to leave every classroom teacher-less for up to 30 or so minutes while all the staff was waiting to be paid; but as far as I remember there were no cases of uproar or accidents.

Sometimes we were not summoned to the paying session, but were told: "Sorry – no money." And then in the staffroom toilet a notice would appear: "Sorry, teachers, no toilet paper. No money."

Carl Gustaf (for size) stands in front of one of the fig trees near Henry Heyring's original home.

Henry Heyring and Decorative Grasses.

Each of the Ethiopian lakes had its own individual beauty and attraction. Lake Zwai was really a vast marsh surrounded by splendid vegetation and soggy terrain that *looked* safe enough until your car was clamped in its formidable, glutinous grip. Lake Helena was the haunt of gigantic tortoises. They didn't mind people sitting or standing on their backs.

Wicked friends took one of the giants back to Addis and then dumped him on us. We let him loose in the garden where, like the pony Tommy, he was addicted to Mother's best Lupins, with which she had hoped to win a prize at the horticultural show. Between them Tommy and Henry – as we named the tortoise – demolished any hopes of Lupin success.

A fence kept Tommy in the back garden but Henry was unstoppable. He simply bulldozed his way to wherever the fancy led him; so it was with some relief that we noticed that, having flattened and munched Mother's flowers and vegetables to nothing, he had crashed through our garden fence into the school compound, which was very large and surrounded by wild bush. (It became bigger and bigger as thieves regularly removed the barbed wire fencing.) No matter how ample the space available to Henry it was always easy to find him. He left a wide trail of compacted vegetation wherever he ambled inside or outside the school grounds; and soon everyone realised that he approved of the football field, which he mowed very effectively. Visiting academics didn't always appreciate being given calculating looks, eye-to-eye, by a huge, self-confident reptile.

Another casualty to Mother's hopes of winning prizes at any horticultural show happened when Amun, one of our horses, fell ill.

As well as medicines we had to give him fresh grass so we took it in turns to go out onto the mountains and cut crisp, salubrious verdure. Amun was recovering nicely when Mother noticed that her large bed of Decorative Grasses, grown from specially imported seeds – her hopes for a win in the Best Bowl Arrangement – had mysteriously vanished.

Christopher, unconscious of Mother's hopes, had enterprisingly saved himself the chore of trudging into wild terrain to find Amun's medicinal grass.

174

Lady of the provinces

175

MATHILDA COOKS THE CURATE.

I have changed names but V. J. and Mathilda lived and were renowned personalities. It was a privilege to have known them.

***

After a long and acclaimed academic career in London, Miss V. J. Reynolds, universally known as V. J., went to Ethiopia to teach in Addis where she would be near her nephew, John. When I knew her, V. J. was rather bent, but she nevertheless nudged eighty with determination. She wore her straight, not-always-pristine, white hair short, and held back by two hopelessly-positioned slides. On her stubby nose she had for years balanced pince-nez, and this had had an unfortunate effect upon her face. The spectacles which were continually slipping, having to be retrieved, and squeezed back onto the long-suffering organ, were attached round her neck by a black string that luckily didn't show the dirt! Her small, square countenance was crossed by such a maze of wrinkles that the nose actually seemed to vanish. I was one of her pupils and, as she peered short-sightedly at us, she reminded me of a tortoise. But old as she was, she never lost her quick intelligence or her sometimes lamentably direct manner that could often be superbly rude.

In those days cars were few and unreliable. Four-footed transport was essential; so V. J. had a well-set-up mule called Mathilda, mottled grey of body with a darker mane and tail. The creature's ears were as soft and as long as any four-hoofed beauty could possibly have desired and she knew perfectly – when she felt like it – how to pick her way most precisely and safely through the rocks and grassy tussocks of any African mountainside. It's true that her eyes held a look that showed she could be obstinate – well – as stubborn as a mule in fact.

This pig-headed paragon – hmm – *almost* paragon – was a gift from a grateful local nobleman when his daughter amazed everyone, including herself, by passing a maths exam that enabled her to enter Nursing School. Mathilda had as good a pedigree as any horse-donkey cocktail could expect. She'd been carefully broken-in and was as well-trained as she condescended to be. The wilful gaze

176

remained, and sometimes her behaviour matched the look. But grooms just shrugged. She was, after all, a mule; and good mules have 'temperament'. In that the new mount was well-matched with her aged and cantankerous owner. V. J. was 'a character', sometimes as wayward as her unexpected acquisition. But she met her match in Mathilda.

The *syce* who delivered the valuable quadruped, gasped with horror when the lady approached his charge from the left: the side from which European riders usually mount. Ethiopians, however, climb onto their steeds from the right, and the lad was sure that Mathilda, being a strong-minded beast, would be displeased by this strange foreign habit. He was right! Never had such a display of kicking, rearing and biting been seen in the precincts of The English School. Nothing would persuade or browbeat the animal to change her habits; so eventually V. J. grudgingly admitted defeat and learnt to mount from the "wrong" side. First victory to Mathilda!

Next it was discovered that V. J.'s four-footed windfall was a racist! – And this at a time when the word wasn't even known, let alone understood! Like the Emperor's pet lions, Mathilda – did – not – LIKE – *foreigners*! She would allow indigenous people to mount (from the right) and she carried them docilely enough – when in a good mood – over many miles of plateaux and mountains. She even deftly negotiated narrow paths up and down steep canyons. But, for the whole of Mathilda's long and bigoted life, any foreigner approaching visibly was doomed to end ignominiously in the mud. V.J. compromised. A strong groom always held the steed's head as her owner crept up stealthily, diagonally from the rear (carefully out of direct line of mulish eyes and hoofs).

This tactic of crabbing up towards Mathilda was not invariably successful as, whether her rider was black, brown, white, yellow or coffee-coloured, at the crucial moment when her aspiring cavalier was most vulnerable, bending to insert a foot into a stirrup, the creature enjoyed wrenching her head out of the groom's grasp. She then gave a good hard nip to the unfortunate rider's derrière. Matty became adept at her timing and the school kids learnt to watch, giggling with anticipation, whenever their teacher tried to rise saddle-wards. Until V. J. had a double patch of stout material stitched to the seat of her jodhpurs she was often rather raw about the nether region.

177

Need I spell out that the incorrigible jade would not accept any saddle other than the traditional high-pommelled, stiff-backed, old, wooden type with tassels, little bells and other ornaments? Presumably she considered that a simple English version would be infra dig! She ruined two valuable European articles by rolling diabolically in slime, mud and on granite. Despite a very sore sit-upon Miss Reynolds was forced to declare (untruthfully) that she was most comfortable in the strange local contraption; so Mathilda kept her posterior-pinching throne. That went with a colourful, jingling bridle boasting ornate cheek leathers, and a complicated harness of red straps over her withers, along her flanks, over her rump and under her tail. Fully 'garbed' she was indeed a noisy and imposing sight!

Mathilda put her ears as far back as possible and rolled her eyes evilly.
Note the tiny Ethiopian stirrup iron made to hold just the big toe. V.J. was able
to change that to a normal stirrup iron without Mathilda being aware of the swap.

Surprisingly, V.J. continued to ride Mathilda, and became deeply devoted to the intransigent beast. Maybe it was because deep

178

called to deep. Or maybe she appreciated that once aloft, with a groom running beside her stirrup in the manner of an aristocratic Ethiopian lady, she could be completely confident of a safe ride. Though more amenable than Mathilda, horses are not as sure-footed as mules, and the old lady needed safe transport. The car-less Vicar had a much more amenable horse to get around his parish, but his curate, Mr Claude Fanning, a painfully shy and raw greenhorn, terrified of anything wearing hoofs, made do with Shank's Pony, and accumulated startling blisters by reluctantly walking great distances to visit his widespread parishioners.

V. J. usually spent holidays with her nephew and his wife on their isolated farm. One year, just before Christmas the curate dutifully hiked out to John's farm to celebrate a pre-Christmas Communion and roast guinea fowl with V.J., her hosts and such of the farm workers who professed to be Christians. He was new to the ministry, new to Africa, unused to a broadly scattered parish, and an excellent example of authorities sending keen beginners to totally unsuitable postings. The tall, mild, young man given to contemplation but *not* keen on foot-slogging, found it particularly agonising covering the nearly thirty miles of African bush to reach John's property. However, being conscientious, he limped on.

On December 23rd Claude sprained an instep. The foot swelled to rhino-esque proportions and was incredibly painful. The Vicar was down with a bad dose of malaria so Claude *had* to get back to town to officiate at the Christmas services. But how could he return in time? There was no car and no road. With his injured instep, walking along shockingly rough footpaths was out of the question.

Worried fumes seemed to spiral from John's locally-made straw hat which, having endured many hardships, was decorated with numerous fraying holes. He lifted the well-ventilated object and scratched his head. All his horses had been sent down for a big job on his lower farm at the bottom of a steep gorge. It would take 24 hours to recall a mount. In his stable at present there was only Mara, who was about to drop a foal at any instant, – and Mathilda!
"Put him on my mule," suggested V. J.

The thought of placing the timid, non-riding cleric on *that* obstreperous back made the farmer sweat! But there was no alternative! Ample padding was lashed to the horrendous saddle. With two men holding the creature's head, two more hanging onto the straps round her rear regions, and a fifth bravely anchoring her tail, the praying pastor was carefully eased onto his charger. Two teams of four stalwarts, each clutching a springy eucalyptus switch, went along to share duties because sometimes persuading Mathilda to move or checking her more outrageous schemes was no joke! John waved them off with bated breath and crossed fingers.

Mr Fanning, with fair-gingery hair and a complexion to match, had a sensitive skin, and not only on the cheeks of his face. Soon Mathilda's terrible saddle rubbed awkward spots of his anatomy painfully raw. Then they came to the river where usually Matty played merry hell. The ford was only knee-deep but predictably refusing to approach the water, she pushed her four stubborn hoofs forward and her tough body backwards. In vain the curate's eight burly escorts pushed, tugged, and even tried to *lift* the mule into the river. Blandishments changed to swearing. Even though the grooms were specialists in local imprecations Mathilda was less than impressed. Kicked and bitten, head-butted and bleeding, the men withdrew to discuss the situation. One bright spark suggested putting burning hay beneath her tail.

The poor, suffering, minister thought he'd been abandoned. Sitting disconsolate on his statue-like mount, he regarded the backward-pointing ears, noted the evilly rolling eyes, and was scared stiff when, every now and again, his courser shivered *all* her skin to emphasise her determination *not* to cross---that---stream! Swirling water filled him with trepidation and extreme revulsion. Moreover, he believed reports that water snakes with backward-pointing fangs, wriggled about in the vicinity, rejoicing in tasty voles, rats, frogs and in even in larger prey. Painful feet and peeling backside, plus horrifying, brown water were bad enough; the idea of communing with serpents and rats was blood-curdling; but the thought of his parishioners arriving at an empty church on Christmas morning was even worse. Trembling, desperately hugging the fearsome pommel, the anxious man spoke unconsciously:
"Come on, Mathilda. *Please!* We *have* to get there."

Defiant ears went even further back. Rebellious eyes projected fury. *Where* was that *ferengi*'s voice coming from? Could *she* be carrying such a devil on her back? Suddenly the accursed steed was a changed creature. She shot into the water. Luckily the support team reacted swiftly. Plying switches frantically and uttering ear-splitting "WHOOH!"'s, swiping the rider as often as they struck the mule, they foiled Mathilda's devilish intentions of rolling in the river or on its slimy banks. Maybe miracles haven't gone out of fashion after all!

Unfortunately the wonderful wadding slipped from the saddle and ended up a sodden mass under Mathilda's belly. She showed her disapproval by bucking. Mr Fanning bore the pinches of the wooden seat stoically but was nearly undone by the violent motion. Discussing pros and cons of disrobing Mathilda to reinstate the padding, the teams were dissuaded by the almost impossible prospect of remounting their charge. Anyway, sitting for hours on sopping pillows would probably have given the rider a horrible cold as well as an even more excoriated backside. For the rest of the way back to town Claude suffered the hard, nipping, wooden saddle without any protection.

In all the shermozzle of thwarting Mathilda's wicked schemes the priest's fine white Panama hat, the gift from a doting mother, was knocked into the flood. Sporting its elegant black headband it floated majestically off on the current. With the mule now proceeding at a hugely satisfactory, if hurtful, jog, no-one was going to run back to the river and try to retrieve the pastor's smart headgear. Some bathing villager downstream might rescue it and wear it at a perky angle to complement his mud-stained rags.

For several hours Mr Fanning's face and ears were therefore subjected to the scorching sun. They were soon as raw and bleeding as he was skinless from his buttocks to his toes. His hands, still frantically clutching the pommel, suffered the same fate. So did his knees for, although John had offered to lend him trousers, he had preferred to stick to his Empire-builders'-style shorts.

The little cavalcade reached town after sunset. Three donkey-loads of hay were bought so that Mathilda wouldn't starve and her carers could enjoy comfortable slumbers in the vicarage stables.

The church had an enormous porch, which was a boon during the Rainy Season: macs could be donned or removed, and umbrellas raised or lowered without any eyes being poked. Here Art College students had set up a realistic, life-sized nativity scene. When the padre, hobbling bow-legged because of his battered bum, raw thighs and skinless feet, limped across from his house to take the Christmas service he found a meditative addition amongst the stable animals. Then he had a shock! It was a mule! – A fiend that he'd never – *ever* – forget! Being a diffident young man he merely uttered a faint:

"Er – Hello, Mathilda. What are *you* doing here?"

The intruder laid her ears so far back that they touched her withers. She lifted sneering lips to bare long teeth in a particularly vicious leer, and glared malevolently at the appalled cleric out of the corners of her eyes:

"Can't you *see?* – I'm enjoying the hay in Baby Jesus' manger?"

With obvious intent she swivelled so that her back was suitably positioned for aggression. Being a little late anyway, the poor pastor decided that discretion was the better part... and tottered into church.

With a strange, painful, rolling gait he staggered up the aisle and turned his glowing, lighthouse-like countenance towards the congregation. The brilliance of his ears almost outdid the decorations of bright red pepper berries that in these climes substituted for holly. During the sermon he was petrified to observe, just behind people in the back row, a pair of long fluffy ears pointing to heaven and apparently absorbing every word. Vee-shaped, they were sending a rude sort-of-Churchillian message!

At the end of the service Claude realised he'd have to pass those ears on his way out of the building. However, the raw young man had grit so, through skinless lips, he managed to wish his flock: "May you all enjoy a Very Merry Christmas" before advancing down the aisle towards his pet hate.

I wish that I could report that Mathilda's experiences converted her. Alas – she remained intractable and pig-headed for the rest of her bigoted life. The curate was delighted to send her back to her owner – together with a dutiful, but lying, letter of thanks for a 'delightful' ride.

182

OTHER BOOKS BY DAPHNE

TRUE adventures:

THROUGH EBOLA TERRITORY
An epic story of an incredible adventure.
In 971 war-torn Zaire, with their new-born son, Bob and Daphne are struggling through overwhelming jungle sometimes with no space between giant trees to erect their tent. Growling deeply, their Land Rover battles through regions where whites have recently been massacred and where people are dying of a mysterious disease – Ebola! Desperate to reach Daphne's parents who are gravely ill in Mallorca, they plough through appalling red ooze that passes for tracks, but they nonetheless enjoy humorous incidents even as they avoid marauding guerrillas, leopards, deadly reptiles and fearsome insects. An official detains Daphne to make her his Wife Number 4 but they escape by floating their Land Rover across a wide river on a raft made from dugouts. Will the young family reach Europe in time for the dying couple to see their new grandson? But will the baby actually survive the gruelling journey?
Lavishly illustrated with Daphne's photos and sketches.

THE DAFTEST JOURNEY
The bulk of the cross-Africa tale.
A trek from south to north across the whole of Africa. At the age of 6 weeks and 12 hours, Bruce sets out, in a fish basket, to traverse the entire continent of Africa. To assist him in this arduous 1971 undertaking he takes with him two slaves: Bob, his father, a Scottish Chartered Accountant, and his mother, Daphne, a university lecturer. The motive power for the fish basket is a short-wheel-based Land Rover, called Pythagoras. Funny/ exciting/ dangerous events come vividly to life as the ***true story*** of ***The Daftest Journey*** unfolds. The little family races death and penury, but battles on from Malawi via Mallorca to Scotland. Conditions are unbelievable, and roads more 'imaginary' than negotiable. They plan to take a boat from Britain to Cape Town, and from there to drive north, back to their home in Malawi. Do they finally make it to their waiting dog? {The Congo crossing is omitted because *Through Ebola Territory* describes that.} Illustrated by Daphne's lively sketches and photos.

GREAT AFRICAN 'RAMBLES' – AND THREE GHOSTS
Gripping stories of fascinating hikes in the wilds of Africa.

Don't be misled by that apparently innocent word 'rambles'. These accounts describe tough climbs: sometimes to oxygen-gasping altitudes, sometimes through jungle, sometimes facing wild animals... all of them in the east of Africa. You don't have to be a mountaineer, or even a walker, to revel in these true tales. Written in Daphne's usual conversational style, they are easily read and will be thoroughly enjoyed by couch potatoes and avid walkers alike.

Daphne tells of her three – yes *three* – varied climbs (1961, 1970, 1986) to the top of Kilimanjaro (the highest point on the African continent), and of the exploits of explorers in past centuries who first tackled that vast dormant, but by no means dead, volcano. She is one of the very few people to have 'rambled' within the snowy, steaming, triple crater of Kilimanjaro.

She takes you into the wilds of the Ruwenzories – also known as The Mountains of the Moon – and you meet 'the Witch of the Woods' when you 'ramble' with Daphne up Meru Mountain. Ma Brown's cottage on Mulange Mountain in Malawi makes a strange appearance.

Complete with three spooky tales of paranormal events that really occurred on Daphne's mountain adventures, this book will keep you enthralled.

The stories sparkle with a host of Daphne's photographs and sketches.

A story based on events that really happened.

FATEFUL FLIES

Fateful Flies tells of dramatic days on one of the vast inland seas in the African Rift Valley. Local inhabitants, flora, fauna and wonderful scenery spring to life; but brutal bandits lurk behind Baobabs. Enthralled at first in a happy, exotic holiday, readers end up chewing their fingernails. The story is based on hair-raising, real-life events that really happened to the author and her son when they lived near the great lake and cruised on it in their GP14 sailing dinghy. Daphne's sympathetic and deep knowledge of the territory and of its fauna, flora and romantic deserted islands, spins a spell that has you

seeing, hearing, and even smelling the experiences that delight or terrify the sailors this book.
Daphne's sketches and photos bring the story alive.

An instructive book

HOW TO ENJOY MAHJONG
It's rare to find such a clear explanation of Mahjong. This excellent book is enhanced by being printed in full colour. The hands, and beauty of the tiles can be appreciated. It's unique in providing photo-copiable spreads of Special Hands and score sheets.

Novels

THE SEER SPOKE
A swastika-studded Who-dunnit underlies a Romance.
Escaping their pasts Craig (a dentist), and art teacher Laura, meet at a Music Society rehearsal in Flauville, a small coastal town in southern France. Why do they resist falling in love? What are they fleeing? AIDS? Bigamy? Murder? Worse? Why is Laura terrified of sex?
Young women and black cats are grotesquely killed at times of full moon. Who is committing the horrific serial slaughter? Who is the frightful Grey Man? Eventual answers are dramatic.

PRE-P.C. AT THE COAST
Here is a vivid, thought-provoking, funny, heart-wrenching picture of life and conditions in some parts of Africa during the 1960s. People who have experienced the spell of the Dark Continent will relish the book's wealth of detail describing situations, scenery, fauna and local atmosphere. You can take this book as a romp or be aware of the economic, ethnic and ecological tensions that it encompasses.

While Kangalia, a newly independent state, teeters between the relative innocence of recent paternal colonial administration and bloody war with a neighbouring country, expatriates live their usual cocooned lives in huge plots along the Indian Ocean coast. Servants of all ages are still 'boys': cook-boy, garden-boy... They still live in 'quarters' on their employers' properties. Roads are potholed dirt; missionaries provide the medical services; and mosquitoes are rampant. Wide, empty beaches of blindingly-white, crushed-coral sands stretch for miles parallel to the reef that froths in emerald waters. Elegant palm tree silhouettes stand black and tall in moonlight bright enough to read by. Among the hills tribesmen practice strange rites, and steamy heat makes expatriate morals go by the board.

Within a big bustling port, shanty town, ramshackle and filthy, is cheek-by-jowl with a stunning, modern airport. Crowded, romantic alleys, winding past picturesque dhows to the seething Souk, and an ancient Fort recall Arab slavers and Portuguese adventurers who dominated in past centuries.

Kathryn, a newly-qualified vet, is doing up her parents' ocean-side house. Next door Rory and wheel-chair-bound Liz are building a Centre where, they hope, handicapped Africans will learn crafts, and by selling their artefacts become empowered to abandon lives of extreme pain and hardship. Suave Alistair, with a beautiful Kangalian secretary, runs a five-star hotel where tourists, arriving by helicopter, rattle over the rag-clad fisherman who, keen to sell his catch, is heaving his dugout from the waves. With an insatiable appetite for sex, Liam works at the hotel.

The book starts gently; but the pace hots up! Guerrilla atrocities upset the calm of golf, bridge, and gossip. As war drums draw frighteningly closer, an exciting and dramatic finale explodes.

Printed in Great Britain
by Amazon

10509717R00112